"I have led you into the land of CARMEL,
to eat the fruit and the best things thereof."

(Jeremias 2, 7.)

OUR LADY OF MOUNT CARMEL
The Incomparable Patroness of the Order of Carmel

MOTHER THERESE
and the
CARMEL of
ALLENTOWN

By

A Sister of the Community

(S. Elizabeth of the Trinity)

FEAST OF OUR LADY OF MOUNT CARMEL
JULY 16, 1949

JEFFERIES AND MANZ
PHILADELPHIA, PENNSYLVANIA

NIHIL OBSTAT

Joseph A. M. Quigley
Censor Librorum

IMPRIMATUR

D. Cardinal Dougherty
Archbishop of Philadelphia

May 16, 1949

First Foundation of the
Cloistered Carmelite Nuns
of the Ancient Observance
in the
United States of America
and the
Life of the First Foundress

Copyright, 1949
Carmelite Nuns of the Ancient Observance
Carmelite Monastery, Allentown, Pennsylvania

Printed in the United States of America

B-CAR   IV
Mo

DECLARATION

Conformably to the Decree of Pope Urban VII, we declare that in the following pages the title of venerable is employed in a purely human sense, and all intention of anticipating the judgment of Holy Mother Church is utterly disclaimed.

"It is of the greatest importance for the soul to exercise itself much in love, so that attaining rapidly to perfection, it may not be detained here below, but may soon see God, face to face."

Saint John of the Cross

LINDENBERG

THE REVEREND MOTHER THERESE OF JESUS, O. CARM.

"From the Heights of Heaven look down on us! See and visit the vine which your right hand has planted, and give it perfection."

PAX ✝ CHRISTI!

In Deepest Gratitude and Filial Veneration
The author Dedicates
This Humble History
To the
BELOVED FOUNDRESSES
of the
CARMEL OF ALLENTOWN
The Reverend
MOTHER THERESE OF JESUS, O. CARM.
and
MOTHER CLEMENT MARY OF THE
GUARDIAN ANGEL, O. CARM.
For the
Greater Honor and Glory
of the
MOST BLESSED TRINITY,
AND HIS
MOST BEAUTIFUL FLOWER
IN THE GARDEN OF HEAVEN,
THE BLESSED VIRGIN MARY OF MOUNT CARMEL!

CONTENTS

PART I

The Order of Carmel

PART II

Mother Therese of Jesus, O. Carm.

CONTENTS

PART III
Carmel of Allentown

PART IV
"Veni, Sponsa Christi!"

MARIA

PREFACE

Feast of the Visitation
July 2, 1949
The Reverend Mother Clement Mary of the Guardian
    Angel, Ord. Carm., Prioress,
Carmelite Monastery
"Saint Therese's Valley"
Allentown, Pennsylvania

Reverend and dear Mother Prioress,

When in October 1925, upon my return to America, on the steamer Columbus, Divine Providence willed that I should meet your venerated Mother Therese of Jesus, the future Foundress of the Carmel of Allentown, I little imagined, at that time, that some twenty years after, I would be privileged to become chaplain at the new Carmel she then was about to found in the new world. Still less did I then think of ever being requested to write a preface to a book, giving a sketch of the life of the saintly Mother.

As you are well aware, Reverend Mother, I hesitated for a considerable time, not only because of my unworthiness to be thus favored, but also because of my incapacity to fulfill adequately your trust. At last, however, I could no longer refuse your wish, considering it to be an act of reverence towards our beloved Mother Therese, as well as a token of personal gratitude for favors I believe to have obtained from Divine Goodness, through her intercession.

One great favor came to me very soon after my arrival at her Carmel, and I am still enjoying it. The other I received at the time of my grave illness, during the winter of 1947, when a patient in the Sacred Heart Hospital, at Allentown. Day and night I wore about my neck the "souvenir" of Mother Therese which you so kindly had given to me, some weeks prior to my hospitalization. Needless to say, it is always with me.

Easter Monday, April 10, 1939, was the memorable day when our dear and regretted Mother's state of health gave much cause for alarm. Aware of her great suffering, one of the nuns lovingly sought to persuade her to remain in bed, and not to go to the Choir for the Holy Sacrifice. The saintly soul, gratefully, yet promptly, replied: "Sister, I would not miss Holy Communion for anything in the world. Tomorrow I shall rest all day." Did she then already have a presentiment of her death on the day following, when "the Lord would lead her

into the land, that floweth with milk and honey"?
(Exod. 13, 5—Introit of Mass on that same day.) Well,
on Tuesday, three hours after the reception of Holy
Communion, the Angel of the Lord announced to her:
"Ite, missa est; depart, now is your dismissal." The
Passion week of Mother Therese's life was over; now
had come for her the triumphant joy of the Eternal
Easter.

It is more than a happy coincidence, that the Introit
of the Mass, at which she had assisted for the last time
in her life, should read thus: "The water of wholesome
wisdom He will give him to drink, alleluja; he shall be
made strong in Him, and he shall not be moved, alleluja;
and He shall exalt him (her) forever, alleluja, alleluja."
(Eccli. 15, 3, 4.)

"The abode of her earthly sojourn was dissolved and
an eternal dwelling place was prepared" for Mother
Therese in heaven, where God exalted His handmaid.
We may well presume that good Mother Therese added
with all her heart, also the words of the Gradual of the
Mass: "This is the day which the Lord hath made; let
us be glad and rejoice therein." (Ps. 117, 24.) "Give
glory to the Lord for He is good: for His mercy endureth forever. Let them say so, that have been redeemed
by the Lord; whom He hath redeemed from the hand of
the enemy, and gathered out of the countries." (Ps.
106, 2.)

XIII

Having received my obedience on July 3, 1947, to repair to the Carmel at Allentown, and take up my new duties as chaplain to the Sisters of our dear Lady of Mount Carmel, I travelled two days later and arrived at Allentown, in the afternoon, shortly before the nuns chanted Vespers. As the taxi driver had stopped the car directly in front of the large public Chapel, I first paid a short visit to the Blessed Sacrament. The interior, as well as the exterior of the Chapel, made a solemn impression upon me. The simple beauty of the sacred edifice easily disposes to devotion.

Because the chaplaincy was still occupied by my predecessor, I was installed in a small apartment, on the second floor of the guesthouse. The inspiring and sweet remembrances of that room I shall never forget. Indeed, my staying there was a rare privilege for me, and a favor, which I shall ever highly esteem. In this room, the venerable Mother Foundress had died. (Before the erection of the new monastery buildings, this apartment had been part of the cloister.)

Near the window, I observed a small table, on which was enthroned, between a pair of candle-sticks, a striking photo of Mother Therese. Within the frame, a printed note read: "In this room, on this spot, our holy Mother Foundress, the Reverend Mother Therese of Jesus, Ord. Carm., breathed her last, on Easter Tuesday morning, at about 10:15 o'clock, April 11, 1939."

At that time, I had known practically nothing about this privileged soul. But there was such a holy and peaceful atmosphere in the little apartment, as one usually imbibes in a Church, wherein the Holy Eucharist is preserved in the tabernacle, or even at the death-bed of a dear friend, whose soul has just taken flight into the Arms of her God. I experienced there, very strongly, the nearness of the Divine, and that of the Mother Foundress.

A little incident which occurred then and there, and which will perhaps better explain my thoughts, I must not omit to mention here. On the first day of my stay, I sat next to the small table, and placed my breviary and handkerchief, for the sake of convenience, on the same table. But, almost immediately, a holy reverence for the place, which I began to consider as a little sanctuary, forced me to remove the objects from the table, and henceforth, nothing could induce me again to place any article thereon. And the thought came to me: That nun is a saint in heaven.

Mother Therese in heaven? We certainly do not wish to forego in any way the judgment of Holy Mother Church. But let us consider her life. To know a person's true character, and to realize its value, we are to study that person in her relation to, and in her daily conduct with her fellow-creatures. Sister Elizabeth's present work, *Mother Therese and the Carmel of Allen-*

town will give us, if not abundant, at least sufficient information about her.

It was really with genuine and much delight, Reverend Mother, and, I assure you, with no less spiritual profit, that I read your daughter's "humble history" concerning your revered Foundress, Mother Therese of Jesus. I did not read the pages of the manuscript all at once, and I purposely abstained from "devouring them," in order to let the various features of the saintly soul's character, so vividly depicted in the sketch, present themselves to my mind, slowly and orderly. But after a careful perusal of the material, it became quite clear to me, that the reasons and motives, which led to its publication, were quite appropriate, and I came to the conclusion that here we have to do with a saintly soul, with a real apostolic woman.

"Give glory to the Lord, for He is good: for His mercy endureth forever." (Ps. 117.) With this verse, the Carmelite priest begins the Holy Sacrifice. These words were ever on the lips and in the heart of good Mother Therese. She lived those words during her earthly pilgrimage; she lived them from her early childhood to her last breath. Her life, as we can easily judge, was entirely spent in the service of the Divine Majesty. Over the cross, on our beloved Mother's grave, the short but precise inscription could be placed: Deum amavit;

she loved God! Or, Confidit in Deo; she trusted in God! Is not this the essential mark that makes a saint?

"A saint," says Tertullian, "is an abridgment of the Gospel." Now, that which makes the Gospel to be what it is, happy tidings, is the Infinite Love of God towards men, which shines forth on every one of its pages. And the aim of the Gospel is, that man should understand this Love, and gratefully return it as much as he can. "Thou shalt love the Lord thy God with thy whole heart and with thy whole soul, and with all thy strength, and with all thy mind; and thy neighbor as thyself." (St. Luke 10, 27.) This is *the* commandment. It is a summary of the entire Gospel. The Christian who faith-fully lives up to it, is a beloved child of God; the Christian who observes it perfectly, has fulfilled the whole law.

The characteristic of Mother Therese's life, it seems to me, consists exactly in her self-surrender to the Infi-nite God, and in her absolute confidence in Divine Provi-dence. On these two pillars she built, with the help of God's grace, her spiritual life as on a solid foundation, and lived her life of faith, love, charity, humility, suffer-ing, poverty, obedience, and chastity. And this her life she lived simply, patiently and gladly; that is, cheerfully.

Surrender of self to the Divine Majesty, reigned as the dominating principle in her; it was the "unum neces-sarium" for her; it was her devotion to God; to this one common denominator she reduced all and everything. Well did Mother Therese understand the words of the Saviour: "He that loveth father or mother more than Me, is not worthy of Me." And, "He that shall lose his life for Me, shall find it." (St. Matth. 10:37, 39.) She realized that God, the absolute Master of all, must occupy the first place in her life; that her little self was but an instrument, a thing in His powerful Hand, and that she had given nothing, if she would not truly empty herself of all that was not God; and thus render herself a vessel, which Christ, "of Whose plenitude we all have received," could fill with His love.

This complete abandonment to God, imparted to her soul that simplicity and unity of life, which only saintly souls enjoy; filled her with that spirit of faith, which made her see all events from a supernatural point of view, which prompted her to judge and to act in the presence of God, "in conspectu Dei," in God and with God. And, as conformity with God's will is a necessary companion of self ⁓ surrender, who should reasonably doubt that she ever submitted her will to that of the Lord, not only praying the petition of the Our Father: "Thy Will be done," but also following it in life?

Her abandonment to God, at last, effected in her that spirit of humility, submission and patience, which we so much admire in her. If she ever felt herself "inclined to nothing," she would give herself to God. Where God is, there is no hardship, no suffering. Or, suffering be comes a privilege, and hence, is taken as a blessing; a burden; yes, but light and sweet . . . love does not suffer!

Thus we readily understand, that everyone and every. thing Mother met with in life, she looked upon as a messenger, a message from God, and received all with charity, equanimity and calmness. In her dealings with the Sisters, as well as with outsiders, and especially with agents and workingmen, she proved to be not only the "mulier fortis"—the "valiant woman," spoken of in the Proverbs, (31, 10) when "many daughters have gath- ered together riches; but she has surpassed them all," (29) — but she showed herself to be also a loving Mother, ever ready to understand, and to help everyone. Sympathies or aversions to souls she knew not, in all she beheld the image of God, the immortal soul, and she loved all on this account.

Yet, with all her activity,—just recall her incessant labors, and sacrifices, before, as well as during and after, the Allentown foundation—Mother Therese ever recog- nized the necessity of prayer, meditation, and recollec- tion, and gave herself, with great love, to these exercises, which after all, are the "best inheritance" of the Car- melite.

We can easily imagine her, after a day of hard toil and labor and sacrifices, drag her tired body to the grille, in the oratory, from which point she could gaze on the tabernacle, and empty her soul before the All-good God, in deep adoration, in the spirit of humility and true contrition, with a loving and trustful heart, asking pardon for her faults, recommending to the Divine Majesty her own soul, the souls of her spiritual daughters, those of all priests and benefactors, the entire Church, and all sinners.

Can we, therefore, be astonished at the greatness of her Confidence in God; to Him she had given her whole self and everything? It is, therefore, only consequent that from His Infinite Power and Goodness, she should hope, too, to receive everything. God Himself taught her how to direct her eyes towards Him, expecting all from Him, thanking Him for everything.

"God will provide," Mother Therese used to say; that was all, and then left everything in God's Hands, things material and things spiritual, her own affairs, as well as those of others who recommended themselves to her prayers, in their troubles.

The servant of God herself, throughout her whole life, was not spared heavy trials, and sufferings of various kinds, including disappointments from the side of such, who by reason of their office should have stood up for her, helped, and defended her. The Lord demanded indeed, more than ordinary sufferences from His handmaid, whom He, however, had well fitted for the taking of His yoke upon herself, by giving her an abundance of favors and graces. She, undoubtedly, also felt the weight of her responsibilities as Foundress and Prioress. Yet, with her unwavering faith, and her blind trust in the Lord's help, as well as her steadfast co-operation with Divine Grace, she could ever say with Saint Paul: "I can do all things in Him, Who strengtheneth me." And as her eyes were always directed towards the Lord, she, in all sincerity, could confess with the Psalmist: "As the eyes of servants are on the hands of their masters; as the eyes of the handmaids are on the hands of their mistress, so I lift up my eyes to Thee, Who dwellest in the heavens." (Ps. 122.)

How appropriately we can apply to her the words of the Prophet, said of Jacob: "The Lord found (him) her in a desert land, in a place of horror, and of vast wilderness: He led her about and taught her: and kept her as the apple of His eye. As the eagle, He spread His wings over her, and has taken her and carried her on His shoulders. The Lord Alone was her leader." (5. Mos. 32: 10-12.) This spirit of childlike confidence never left her, not even at times when she seemed to be forsaken by heaven. It ever accompanied her till her death. "O God, let me never be put to shame; for Thou art my rock and my stronghold; and for Thy Name's sake, Thou wilt lead me and guide me. Thou wilt bring me out of the net, which they have hidden for me; for Thou art my refuge." (Ps. 30; 1-6.)

The traits of resoluteness, cheerfulness, and calm confidence in Divine Providence we behold in the very features of the servant of God. They indicate nothing of
fear, anxiety, or deceitfulness. Hers was a frank and
optimistic character. Her pleasing disposition, too,
attracted, and hardly anyone of those whom Mother
Therese asked for a favor, could withstand her request.
The non-realities in life did not bother her. She faced
the realities, as they presented themselves to her now
and then, prudently reflected, then decided and acted
with all confidence in the good God.

Does not Mother Therese's life, in some respects bear
resemblance to that of her heavenly protectress, Saint
Theresa of Avila, whose name she also had taken, and
whose maxims she had made her own?

> "Let nothing disturb thee. Let nothing affright thee.
> All things are passing; God only is changeless.
> Patience gains all things. Who hath God wanteth nothing—
> God *Alone* sufficeth."

Blessed are the dead, who die in the Lord henceforth.
Yes, says the Spirit, let them rest from their labors, for
their works follow them." (Apoc. 14.) Mother Therese
lived in the Lord. A truly interior soul she was, undivided and one, whose life was a "hidden one in Christ."
A nothing she wanted to be before God; "He must increase, but I must decrease," (St. John, 3; 30); and
therefore, forgetting herself, she sought God alone . . .

A secret martyrdom was her life, but there reigned in her soul the "Pax Christi in Regno Christi." The Peace of Christ lived in her, because the Kingdom of Christ was within her, and in that kingdom she was ever the humble handmaid of her King Jesus. Now her soul rests in eternal peace, and reigns with Christ, the King of Peace!

"Fear not, little Flock, for it hath pleased the Father to give you a Kingdom." (St. Luke, 12; 32.) "To-morrow I shall rest all day." Thus she spoke on Easter Monday, 1939, when one of the nuns had asked her to have a little mercy with her body. On Easter Tuesday, the Divine Gardener transplanted His flower, from her earthly Carmel (garden of God), to the celestial Carmel on high.

Having taken her flight, the venerable Mother Therese of Jesus has not altogether left us. As her mortal remains peacefully repose within the holy sanctuary of the cloister, so also dwells her spirit, with her zealous daughters, in the Carmel of Allentown. Her spirit lives on . . . For of her it *cannot* be said, that she belonged to those "of whom there is no memorial; that they are perished, as if they had never been born." (Eccli. 44, 9.) No, of her truly may be said, that "the Lord hath wrought great glory," that "she has left a name behind her, that her praises might be related." "She was a

woman of mercy, whose godly deeds have not failed."
"Her body is buried in peace, and her name liveth unto
generation and generation." (Eccli. 44; 2-14.)

"Her name liveth" not only with her spiritual
daughters, inside the cloister of Carmel, but it is also
in the mind and heart of a host of outsiders, people of
all ranks of society, who knew her well, and were
attracted to God by her spirituality and her virtues.
Many effectively had asked her prayers while she was
alive, and many more since, have attested that they have
received graces and favors from heaven, through her
intercession. Sister Elizabeth has listed a number of them
in her "history."

We may surmise that Mother Therese, is a beloved
friend of God, whom He wishes to be a channel through
which His Goodness bestows blessings on us! And it
seems to me, that God has special designs in making
known to us the life of this humble nun.

It is providential, that at a time of universal disorder,
hatred, greed, discontentment, strife and fear; at a time,
when craving for the goods of this world seems to take
all love of God away from the hearts of many; at a time
when it takes even many good Christians so long a time,
perhaps a life-time, to become actually conscious and
personally convinced of the saving truth, that the greatest happiness for man on earth is to seek and love God;
at a time, I say, when cloistered life is not a little criti-

cized for its "inactivity and unsuitableness," God should raise another soul from the cloister, to teach others by her example how to combine effectively, a life of prayer with a life of work, and in a manner pleasing to Him "so as to pass through the good things of the present, as not to lose those of eternity," (Prayer of the Mass on the 3rd Sunday after Pentecost), being "a doer and not only a hearer of the word."

Let all, therefore, take up this "humble history," learning from it to seek and find rest in God, while having the favorite saying of our saintly Mother, in their hearts and on their lips: "Thou, O God, hast created our heart for Thee, and it is restless, until it rests in Thee." (St. Aug. Conf. Ch. 1.) May the Divine Master and the glorious Queen of Carmel, deign to bless it, and all those who read it and regard its lessons.

I thank you once more, Reverend and dear Mother Prioress, for the manuscript you so kindly gave me to peruse. We are greatly indebted to the author, Sister Elizabeth of the Trinity, whose pen has produced, in so simple but clear style, a knowledge of this privileged soul.

The "humble History" of Mother Therese is timely indeed. Undoubtedly, the book will do much good to all classes of souls also outside the cloister or convent. May it be to all readers a holy incentive to love the good God as He deserves to be loved.

You, Reverend Mother, as the intimate and constant companion of the saintly Foundress, were favored to gain a thorough knowledge of her pious character, a grace for which you are ever grateful to Divine Goodness. Your spiritual daughters in Carmel, especially those who were closely associated with the Reverend Mother Therese, share your gratitude. The highest tribute, however, we can pay to the holy Foundress, is the walking in her spirit. May it inspire all Carmelites with new zeal in the execution of their sublime calling.

I bless you, Reverend Mother Clement Mary, as well as the Sisters under your care, and remain

Your humble servant in Christ Jesus
and the Holy Virgin Mary,

Fr. Simon Maria Schmitt, O. Carm.

Whitefriars Hall,
Carmelite Theological Seminary,
Washington, D. C.

The Carmelite Seal — Its Symbolism

Upon Carmel's Escutcheon you see a mountain in brown, and three golden stars, in a field of white: above, a fiery sword over a crown, and the motto: "ZELO ZELATUS SUM PRO DOMINO DEO EXERCITUUM." (With zeal have I been zealous for the Lord God of Hosts.) Herein, the spirit and history of Carmel are symbolically expressed. The mountain denotes MOUNT CARMEL, the reputed birthplace of the Order, and for many centuries its Home. It also denotes the spirit of contemplation and prayer, peculiar to Carmel. The fiery sword of Elias, over MARY'S diadem, Carmel's crowning glory, signifies the spirit of zeal for GOD, and for OUR LADY. Both combined, prayer and zeal, constitute that double spirit of Elias, —the spirit of CARMEL. The three golden stars stand for the three epochs of the Order's history, the Prophetic, the Greek, and the Latin.

The Holy Prophet ELIAS, wrapt in prayer, on Mount Carmel, beholds the small cloud, prefiguring the Immaculate Virgin Mother of God, who would give to the world the promised Messias.

PART I

The Order of Carmel

"Come apart, for a while, and rest on the serene shores of MOUNT CARMEL. Hearken to the voices from the holy Mountain,—the voices that speak of *love,* and of *prayer,* and particularly, the gracious voice of the Peerless Mother of Carmel!

May you drink deeply of its refreshing peace, its sacred calm, that your soul may be filled with the divine atmosphere of Carmel. And there, in the sublimity of peace, contemplate the sweetness of your GOD."

1

Carmel — Its Origin and History

THERE IS A holy enchantment in the name CARMEL, seemingly austere, yet beautiful and tender. We spontaneously want to know something about the CARMELITE ORDER, one of the older orders in the Church of God, outstanding for its unique traditions and its history.

What is the meaning of CARMEL? Geographically speaking, by Carmel we mean the "Carmel by the sea," mentioned in the Book of Josue, Ch. 19; 26, in contradistinction to another mountain of the same name, situated in the south of Palestine.

In Hebrew, CARMEL signifies "Garden, or Vineyard, of God." And MOUNT CARMEL is famous just because of its fruitfulness. In the Sacred Books of the Old Testament its majesty and beauty are extolled. Its perennial green and luxurious fertility have made it the most attractive place in the Holy Land, even to this very day. While on most mountains in Palestine there is hardly a tree visible, Mount Carmel is studded with trees and shrubbery. The climate there is very moderate. Rich rains fall in winter and thus keep the earth moist

3

for the greater part of the year. In March and April we see the Mount don its festival garment. Thousands and tens of thousands of sap-green oak and olive trees appear in their venerable splendour, in their bloom of youth. The surface of the sacred soil, however, is covered with an immensely large carpet of flowers of many, many kinds. In the less inhabited parts we find even fig, almond, apricot and pomegranate trees, and in still more isolated spots precious aromatic and medicinal plants and herbs lie hidden like a treasure. A gorgeous sight to behold, this CARMEL in the Holy Land, "God's Garden."

CARMEL is not a single mountain as, for example, Mount Tabor. It is a chain of mountains, in great part of limestone, stretching from southeast to northwest for a distance of about fifteen miles (or, six hours walk), having a width that varies from three to five miles, and a maximum height of about eighteen hundred feet. At its northwestern extremity, it majestically overlooks the tranquil blue waters of the Mediterranean Sea on one side, forming the picturesque Promontory. On the other side, to the southeast, a superb view of the plain of Esdralon can be enjoyed from its highest point, called Muhraqa, the sacred site of the Sacrifice of great Prophet Elias. At the foot of the mountain lies the modern city of Haifa with the new harbor, prostrate as in adoration of the Creator-God.

In Holy Scripture CARMEL appears, above all, as a type of *spiritual* fruitfulness. Thus we read in the Canticle of Canticles: "Thy head is like Carmel" (7; 5); and in Isaias: "The beauty of Carmel is given to her" (35; 2). These words refer to the mystical fertility and beauty of the soul redeemed, to Christ's spouse—His Church, and eminently to the Immaculate and ever Blessed Virgin Mother, MARY, whom we invoke under the sweet titles of "Mater, Decor Carmeli," Mother, Ornament of Carmel; "Virgo, Flos Carmeli," Virgin, Flower of Carmel.

Since time immemorial CARMEL has been considered a Holy Mount, a sacred temple where the Deity was revered. Not only for Hebrews, but even for pagans it was a place for recollection, prayer, and sacrifice. "Between Judea and Syria is the Carmel; thus is called the mountain and the god." (Tacit. Hist. 2; 78). In the life of the celebrated philosopher Pythagoras of the second century before Christ we read that he often went to meditate "in the sacred place of Carmel." Of Jamblichus, his biographer, likewise a Grecian philosopher, we are told that "he landed at Sidon, and then proceeded to the Carmel to visit the sanctuary on this mountain." Similar testimonies are found in Tacitus and Suetonius, speaking of Vespasian before he went to war against the Jews. He consulted the oracle, which was on one of Carmel's tops (Tacit. Hist. 2; 78).

Sanctuary, altar and place of oracle were probably destroyed when the kings of Israel led the people away from the true God.

Yet, what made Carmel forever famous was the sojourn upon it of the great Thesbite (Thesba in Western Palestine was Elias' birthplace) ELIAS and his faithful successor Eliseus, and the miraculous happenings there. Eliseus was at Carmel when a weeping mother came and begged him to go to Sunam and call back to life her only son, who had died of a sunstroke (4. Kings 4; 17-37). On certain days the faithful children of Israel used to go up to Carmel to pray, offer sacrifice and consult the prophets.

The central figure of Carmel, however, is ELIAS. To this very day the Mount in the language of the people is called "Jabal Mar Elias," the Mountain of Saint Elias. Christians, Moslems and Jews alike venerate him. Elias signifies "Lord God," or "God reigns." And most appropriately is he called by this name, for Elias made it his life's program "to be zealous for the Lord, God of Hosts" (3. Kings 19; 14). During the deepest degradation of Israel under the godless Achab and his pagan queen Jezebel, Elias alone stood up as fearless witness to the faith in the one true God, and as staunch defender of the Law. Chapters seventeen and eighteen of the Third Book of Kings give glorious testimony of the zeal and power this greatest among the ancient prophets of Israel displayed on Carmel.

The noblest hymn of praise is sung to him also, in the beginning of Chapter forty-eight of the Book of Ecclesiasticus. "Thus was Elias magnified in his wondrous works. And who can glory like to thee?" Expressively and beautifully at one and the same time this praise of Elias is re-echoed in the solemn preface on his feast, celebrated in the Carmelite Order on July 20th. Let us quote it for the sake of the many who have never heard it: "It is meet indeed and just, right and helpful unto salvation, always and everywhere to give thanks to Thee, Holy Lord, Father Almighty, eternal God, and on the Solemnity of Blessed Elias, Thy prophet and our Father, to bless and praise Thee with joyful minds. Who in Thy word stood up as a fire; shut the heaven; raised up dead men; broke the tyrants' power in pieces; destroyed the sacrilegious and laid the fundaments of monastic life. Who by angelic ministry was refreshed with food and drink and walked in the strength of that food unto the Holy Mountain. Who was taken up in a whirlwind and will be the Forerunner of the second Advent of Our Lord Jesus Christ . . . "

"Forerunner of the second Advent of Our Lord Jesus Christ." Who of us is not reminded here of the Gospel of the second Sunday of Lent telling the story of the Transfiguration of Our Lord and the glorious apparition

of Moses and ELIAS with Christ? Elias, we say, because it was prophesied by Malachy that he (Elias)
would be sent to prepare the way for the Redeemer.

Again, in his Catholic Epistle, Saint James the
Apostle (5; 17) lauds him as a man of prayer, to make
clear his assertion that the persevering prayer of the just
man profits much. "Elias," says Saint James, "was a
mortal man like ourselves: and with prayer he prayed
that it might not rain upon the earth. And it rained not
for three years and six months. Then he prayed anew.
And the heaven gave rain; and the earth brought forth
her fruit." Truly, not only did Elias call fire from
heaven upon his sacrifice, thus proclaiming the victory
of God and confounding the idolatrous priests of Baal,
but by his assiduous prayer he also stopped the famine.

"And behold, a little cloud arose out of the sea, like a
man's foot, and there fell a great rain" (3. Kings 18; 44).

The cloud that appeared in the clear sky after a long
drought, and which announced to the people the coming
of the precious and long desired rain, has been looked
upon by a number of Fathers of the Church as a type
of the Most Blessed Virgin Mary, Who bore within
Herself, as the cloud bears water, the Author of all
grace, the Principle of all fruitfulness, JESUS CHRIST,
the world's Holy Redeemer. Well, then, do we salute
MARY as OUR LADY of MOUNT CARMEL.

Whether our Holy Father Elias saw in the cloud a

8

figure of the future HOLY MOTHER of GOD, or no, is it of any consequence? What reason, however, could prohibit us from cherishing the belief, and adhering to the tradition of the Carmelite Order, that especially the disciples of the prophets, and other dwellers on Carmel and elsewhere, who walked in the steps of Elias and Eliseus, were, in their own way, devoted to that Virgin of whom Isaias in the eighth century before Christ had foretold: "Behold a Virgin shall conceive and shall bring forth a son, and his name shall be called Em-manuel" (Is. 7)? And would it be fair to assume that our holy Leader, Elias, or his followers were unaware of the very first promise of the world's Redeemer, found on the first pages of Holy Writ: "I will put enmities between thee (serpent) and the woman (Mary), and thy seed and her seed: she shall crush thy head, and thou shalt lie in wait for her heel" (Gen. 3; 15)? And Elias was so zealous for God's glory and the salvation of souls. For this reason also, as representative of the Prophets, he was accounted worthy to offer homage to the Messiah on the Mount, and to speak with Him and discourse with Him concerning His Passion and Death, which Christ was soon to offer for the salvation of the world. In the same way, it is not excluded that he, whose very name reveals his mission, after his being translated from this world, should have heard secrets about the Virgin, told to no one else.

9

In such sense we speak of veneration of the Mother of the Messiah to come, on the part of those men of God, who from the time of Elias to the time of the Holy Saviour and down to our own days, have been serving God in "the school of the Prophet." We refer here to the monks of Carmel, commonly called Carmelites.

And similarly we also regard the renowned Prophet Elias as our holy Father and Leader. For there have always been those whose aspiration and privilege it is to follow his example of constantly, "day and night," living in God's Presence, and leading a life of contempt of the world and conversation with the Divine.

Moreover, it is more than probable that early monasticism celebrated in Elias its Old Testamentic Leader. We therefore do not find it strange, either, to read in the fourth lesson of the Divine Office on the Feast of our dear Lady of Mount Carmel that the followers of Elias were among the first to embrace the Christian faith, after our Blessed Redeemer had come to bring to the world the happy tidings of His Kingdom.

Thus we see that the Order of Carmel has a history altogether its own, and clings to the very old and venerable tradition that the religious life, hermitical as well as cenobitic, continued to flourish upon Mount Carmel so as to make an uninterrupted succession from the time of the Prophet Elias down to the "foundation" of the Order as effected in the thirteenth century. There is no other order in the Church which claims such privilege.

It is obvious that Elias is not considered Founder in the sense in which Saint Benedict is the Founder of the Benedictines, or Saint Francis the Founder of the Franciscans, and others the founders of their respective religious families. However, Pope Benedict XIII in 1725 did grant the Order the privilege to erect the statue of Saint Elias in Saint Peter's at Rome, with the inscription below: "Erected by the entire Order of Carmel to Saint Elias its Founder." And it occupies the first place among the other founders.

To state exactly the time when Carmelite "hermiticism" or monasticism spread in the first thousand years after Christ is difficult. It cannot be ascertained historically, as convincing sources fail. About the year 412, John, Patriarch of Jerusalem, is said to have provided the "monks" of Carmel with a rule.

The following account, based upon reliable sources, is of no small interest. Probably none of our kind readers has ever visited the ancient dwellings of the monks on Carmel. Reference is not made here to where the Carmelite Monastery with its grand Basilica dedicated to Our Lady of Mount Carmel now stands on the Promontory; no, an hour or so away, in the backwoods where the modern traveler or pilgrim does not step. You perhaps have read that Carmel's sides, still so green and fresh, are furrowed by many valleys, and burrowed by very numerous grottos, which in olden times afforded a safe refuge to those who were fleeing from justice, or persecution. Allusion to this fact is made by the prophet Amos: "And though they hid in the top of Carmel I will search and take them away from thence" (9; 2). These places, so eminently suited also to the contemplative life, naturally drew to themselves Christian anchorites (hermits) at an early age.

From the Basilica, situated at a height of 450 feet, we descend the mountain side and direct our steps southwards. After an hour's walk, we reach the entrance of a fertile valley. The Arabs call it Wadi Siyah, that is, the Valley of the Hermits. It also bears the name of the Valley of the Cascade of Elias, because the Elias Fountain is there. This valley has been hallowed by Christian hermits from the earliest ages of the Church, and there lived our saints and martyrs. Those hermits had received a rule already in the fifth century, as mentioned above. As has been historically proved, there was a monastery there in 570, "the monastery of Eliseus the Prophet, on the spot where he was met by the woman whose son he raised," (Antonino of Piacenza). The traces of that monastery can still be seen. Nearby is the Fountain of Elias, and here we have to look for the Hermitage of Saint Eliseus with the remnants of the caves formerly inhabited by religious. They are numerously scattered through the valley; even "beds" and "windows" in the projecting rocks are observable. With right do the natives call that district Shif Arruhban, that is, Cave of the Monks. And where the valley branches out, there used to be a monastery in honor of Saint John, the "second Elias." Today we find a small village there, whose name testifies to this fact. To this day it has the name Id Deir, Monastery.

Jacques de Vitry, (1210), when speaking of the Carmelites, says that "one of the convents, situated near the Fountain of Elias and inhabited by men who copy the virtues of the Prophet, was dedicated to Saint Margaret. There is a chapel in the rock." Of this monastery we still witness the ruins that belong to the most ancient monuments of Christian archaeology. The monks therein undoubtedly followed the (Greek) Byzantine Rite, at least the great majority, which fact accounts for their dedicating their convent to Saint Margaret.

After the twelfth century we notice a decided change in the management and affairs of the "order." This was due in great measure to the Crusades. After the conquest of Palestine by the Christians (1100), not a few of the Crusaders who decided to remain in the Holy Land and serve God in religion joined those monks on Carmel. One of them was the Crusader Berthold of Limoges in France. (1150.)

This hermit was chosen by Divine Providence to be an instrument in collecting the Latin hermits of the Holy Mountain into a religious community after the manner of the orders of the Latin (Roman) Church. His labours were greatly facilitated by the help of Aimericus, Apostolic Delegate and Patriarch of Antioch, who was Berthold's uncle and who had the interest of the hermits deeply at heart. Later Berthold, with the consent of the brothers, was chosen Superior and took the title of Prior General, a distinction by which the heads of the orders in the West were known. He built for his monks a common abode near the oratory and Fountain of Elias, close to the abbey of Saint Margaret, "a very beautiful and delightful place, where dwell the Latin hermits called the brothers of Carmel, where is also a Chapel of Our Lady, and everywhere on this spot is an abundance of waters, that flow from the rock of the mountain." This interesting account of the first Carmelite Monastery of the style of the West has been handed down to us from the first half of the thirteenth century.

Saint Berthold directed the brothers of Carmel for forty-five years that were full of sufferings endured from the infidels. He reached the venerable age of one hundred and fifteen years.

To consider Saint Berthold as founder of the Order, however, is incorrect, as Berthold himself had joined the institute already in existence. But he gave it a new mold,

14

forming its members into a regular Carmelite Community.

Saint Berthold was followed by Saint Brocard, who had been born of French parents in Jerusalem. Under his direction the number of the hermits of Carmel increased considerably. His holy and exemplary life, as well as that of his predecessor, had caused more and more vocations. In 1207 he begged Albert, Apostolic Delegate and Patriarch of Jerusalem, to make for them a new rule of life, which petition the latter granted "to our beloved Son Brocard and the beloved brother ' hermits living under his obedience near the Fountain of Elias on Mount Carmel." It was approved by Pope Honorius in 1226. This, on the whole, is the rule the Carmelites yet follow today.

Saint Brocard, too, had built a monastery near the smaller fountain, erroneously called the Fountain of Elias, which is still in possession of the Carmelite Fathers.

Among the great saints of the Order who lived at that time on Carmel we mention especially the wonder-worker, Angelus, born at Jerusalem of Jewish parents, and Saint Simon Stock, of English birth, the sixth and best known General of the Order, to whom Our Blessed Lady presented the Holy Scapular.

At an early date (1238) the monks were attacked by bands of Mohammedans. In 1260 many fell victims on account of their faith. After the capture of Acre by the Mohammedans in 1291—Jerusalem had already fallen in 1240—the monks who were unable to escape were mercilessly killed, and the monastery was destroyed. The chapel of Our Lady in the Valley of the Martyrs remained abandoned from that time on. Attempts to repeople Carmel were in vain. The difficulties caused by the Mohammedans were unsurmountable. Thus no monks lived on the Sacred Mountain for three hundred years. In 1631 the Order tried again to gain footing, and Father Prosper of the Holy Ghost, a Carmelite of Spanish extraction, took up his abode with two brothers amid the ruins of the ancient monastery. But they were unable to endure the vexations of the neighboring Mohammedans and departed. In 1767 the Order returned and established a new monastery on the top of the Promontory. This convent was burned by the Mohammedans, the monks and soldiers having been massacred, after Napoleon had left the country (1799). In 1827 the foundation stone of the present monastery was laid, and three or four years later the Carmelites took possession again of the Holy Mountain to sing the praise of God and of the Virgin Mother.

MIGRATION TO THE WEST

When there was no longer any hope of dwelling on the holy Mountain, the Carmelites looked to the West for refuge. As early as 1238, many of their number set sail for Europe, going into Cyprus, and to Sicily. In 1241, several Carmelites arrived in England where the Order spread rapidly, and soon passed into Ireland and Scotland. In 1245, Saint Louis of France opened a Monastery for the Carmelites in Paris. From this House, chiefly, the Order spread through France and Germany. Foundations also multiplied in Spain and in Italy.

Thus did this celestial Vine of CARMEL extend its branches throughout all Christendom, under the maternal protection of the Most Glorious Virgin MARY, who ever has been solicitous to defend, and to preserve the Order which she has honored with her own Name. Pope Urban VII granted an Indulgence to all who spoke of CARMEL as "MARY'S ORDER."

Even though the ensuing list is far from complete, we shall attempt to name some of the Carmelite Saints who shed lustre on the ORDER of CARMEL during this era.

Saint Simon Stock, General of the Carmelites, receives the Brown Scapular from Our Lady of Mount Carmel, on July 16, 1251, at Cambridge, England.

CHAPTER TWO

Saint Simon Stock

OUTSTANDING ON the list of Carmelite saints is Saint Simon Stock, the poet-saint of Carmel in England. It was to Saint Simon that Our Lady was pleased to give a glorious proof of her special love for CARMEL. In 1245, Saint Simon Stock was elected General of the Carmelite Order, and governed it until his death in 1265.

THE BROWN SCAPULAR

On July 16, 1251, at Cambridge, England, the Queen of Carmel, Holy Mary, in heavenly splendour, appeared to the venerable Saint Simon. Burdened by the weight of years, and oppressed by the difficulties encompassing his Order on every side, Simon supplicated the Mother of Carmel to have pity on Her Order in this hour of trial. Thus he prayed during the long night. Part of his petition was expressed in sweetest poetry:

"Flower of Carmel! Blossoming Vine!
Splendour of Heaven! Mother Divine!
None like to Thee.
Mother of Meekness! Peerless and Fair!
Thy children of Carmel, save from despair,
Star of the Sea!"

19

The bountiful Heart of God's Mother could not resist the prayers and tears of the General of Her Order. Towards morning, just as the dawn was breaking, She appeared to the holy man. The sight was entrancing. Surrounded by a great company of angels, of dazzling brightness, the Glorious Queen of Heaven, in answer to his prayer, presented to Simon, the BROWN SCAPULAR, and said these words: "This shall be a privilege for thee, and for all Carmelites; whosoever shall die wearing it, shall not suffer everlasting fire."

From thence, a most wonderful change took place in the Order. Saint Simon, too, was fortified by this celestial vision, and exhorted his brethren to live worthy of such a precious gift, and by good works to make their lives conformable to that of the true servant of MARY. They were to be faithful children of Hers, and ardent servants of Her Divine Son.

The Sabbatine Privilege

Seventy-one years later, the Holy Mother of God added another privilege to this extraordinary favor, namely: The SABBATINE PRIVILEGE, granted through Pope John XXII. Having appeared to Pope John XXII, Our Lady promised that She would assist and console the children of Carmel, detained in Purgatory, and also, speedily release them, especially on the *first Saturday* after their death. Hence the name, *Sabba-tine Privilege*.

Father Elias Magennis, O. Carm., whom we so frequently quote, inserts the authentic transcript of the Sabbatine Bull, wherein Pope John gives his own account of the Vision, in his masterly book, *The Sabbatine Privilege of the Scapular*.

The Sabbatine Privilege has the approval and confirmation of the Popes, and the acceptance by the Church, in the Solemn Office of Our Lady of Mount Carmel.

Carmel's Saints of the Medieval Period

After Saint Simon Stock, we have Blessed Nicholas of France, who succeeded the former as General of the Order. Then, we have Blessed Hilary, and Saint Angelus, who in Rome met Saint Dominic and Saint Francis. Blessed Radulph of Germany, who served as General for a time is also in our number, with Blessed Franco, and the beloved Saint Albert of Sicily, and also Saint Theodoris, Provincial of Germany, who was known for his tender devotion to the Blessed Sacrament. Add to this list Saint Anthony of Offen, who died a martyr in 1399; Blessed Avertano and Saint Romeo, and especially outstanding, Saint Peter-Thomas, one of the greatest glories of the Church of France. It was to this great Carmelite that MARY made the promise, celebrated in the Annals

21

of Her Order: "Peter, fear nothing! The Order of Carmel will last until the end of time." Then followed Blessed John Soreth, who was unanimously elected General of the Carmelites, in 1451. This great man was one of the most eminent Priests of the Church.

Carmelite Nuns

During his Generalship, Blessed John Soreth organized the Carmelite Sisterhoods, and the first Convent of Carmelite Nuns was formally founded at Guelder, Holland, on October 14, 1453. It must be mentioned here, however, that long before this time, pious women were affiliated with the Order of Carmel, as, for example, Blessed Angela of Bohemia, Blessed Jeanne of Toulouse, in 1268, and her companion, Anne of Toulouse.

Blessed John Soreth established another Convent of Carmelite nuns in Liege, in 1463, over which he placed Blessed Frances d'Amboise, former Duchess of Brittany, who shed new lustre on the Order of Carmel, by the holiness of her life. Another contemporary of Blessed Frances, was Blessed Joan Scopelli, who died in the odour of sanctity, on July 9, 1491, in Italy.

All in all, Blessed John Soreth founded five Carmels for nuns. He was a true servant of the Blessed Virgin Mary of Mount Carmel, and when death approached, his last words were directed to his Heavenly Mother:

"O Queen of my heart, I am going to see thee, to possess thee!"

Many Carmelites have succeeded in attaining the highest degree of sanctity under the inspired Rule. But, perhaps, the best known are Saint Teresa of Avila, Saint Mary Magdalen di Pazzi, Saint John of the Cross, and Saint Therese of the Child Jesus.

The Child Jesus appears to Saint Teresa in the Courtyard of the Carmel. His gentle answer sweetly told her: "I am Jesus of Teresa."

CHAPTER THREE

Saint Teresa of Avila

PERHAPS THE most distinguished General of the Carmelites since the time of Blessed John Soreth, was John Baptist Rubeo (Rossi), who permitted the extension of the Teresian Reform in Spain.

The great Saint Teresa of Avila inaugurated the Reform of the Spanish Carmels, on August 24, 1562, in the little Monastery of Saint Joseph, in Avila, with the approbation of Pope Pius IV. The Saint revived the Rule, enjoining strict poverty, and great austerity—above all, the contemplative life of Carmel, and missionary zeal, by prayer and apostolic work. It was she who zealously promoted the Order's time-honored devotion to Saint Joseph, so that it has been affirmed that the great Patriarch owes glory on earth to Saint Teresa.

She was born on March 28, 1515. At twenty years of age, she entered the Convent of the Incarnation, in Avila, which housed one hundred and eighty nuns. Teresa sought untiringly to walk the ways of the mystical life. Gifted with a brilliant mind, she wrote masterpieces of literature. Not without reason has she been named "the greatest of mystics." It would be impossible here to enter into a consideration of her life of prayer and mysticism. As a matter of fact, this eminently practical nun was literally consumed by the love of God.

Let us relate one of the quotations from the Book of her LIFE, in which she describes one of her visions:

"Our Lord was pleased that I should have at times a vision of this kind: I saw an angel close by me, on my left side, in bodily form . . . He was not large, but small of stature, and most beautiful—his face burning, as if he were one of the highest angels, who seem to be all on fire: they must be those whom we call cherubims.

"I saw in his hand a long spear of gold, and at the iron's point, there seemed to be a little fire. He appeared to me to be thrusting it at times into my heart, and to pierce my very entrails; when he drew it out, he seemed to draw them out also, and to leave me all on fire, with a great love of God. The pain was so great, that it made me moan; and yet, so surpassing was the sweetness of this excessive pain, that I could not wish to be rid of it."

After the Saint's death, it was found that her heart was actually pierced. Her body is preserved incorrupt to this day, in the Convent Church of Alba in Spain, and, on the feast of the Transpiercing, her heart is exposed for the veneration of the faithful.

Worn out with her enormous labors, having founded thirty-two convents, and having endured a painful illness with most exemplary patience, she died on October

4, 1582. In her last moments, she saw our Divine Lord, surrounded by angels, waiting to receive her soul. Before and after her death, God glorified His faithful servant, by the working of many miracles.

—Teresa of Jesus—

(An episode in her life)

(These verses were found among the papers
of Mother Therese.)

The midnight chimes have died away,
    The convent aisles are still;
No more the tones of chanted prayer
    Mount Carmel's cloisters fill.

No sound breaks on the dreamlike calm
    Round Jesus' Altar-Throne,
Where, wrapt in wordless ecstacy,
    Teresa kneels alone.

The weird dim shadows of the night
    That o'er the bannered walls,
And wreathes in gloom the niched saints
    And sombre oaken stalls.

The tabernacle star sheds forth
    Its faint, unsteady beams,
That tremble round the "Mother-Queen"
    In show'rs of pearly gleams.

The moon-rays through the columned aisles
    Their spectral measures keep,
And still Teresa kneels in prayer
    For lettered words too deep!

Her hands are clasped; her glorious eyes
    Athwart her veil's dark shroud,
In pure resplendent beauty beams
    like star-lights from a cloud!

The smile that hovers on her lips
    Is born of Heaven and prayer,
The halo on her pale, young face
    A Seraph's brow might wear.

The hours steal away unknown,
    For love seeks not their flight;
And love surpassing human thought,
    That great heart floods tonight.

The love that burned her life away,
    That caused her passioned cry,
While Carmel's thorny heights she scaled,
    "To suffer or to die."

But, lo, a form breaks on the gloom!
    Amid the chancel stands
A fair young Boy, with flowing hair,
    And shining feet and hands.

His mien is soft and grave, His brow
  Is pure as new-born snow,
And wondrous gems of ruby sheen
  O'er all His raiment glow.

"And who art Thou," Teresa asks,
  "And what Thy name, fair Child?"
"My Name?" He answered, and His Voice
  Was low, and sweet, and mild.

"Nay, tell me first what thou art called!"
  Teresa's limpid eyes
Flash forth her soul's deep, rapturous love,
  As swift to Heaven they rise.

"Teresa of Jesus—it is writ
  Upon my longing heart
In characters of light and flame
  By Seraph's burning dart.

"For Him I live, for Him I die,
  My only Love and Joy;
Now speak, and tell me, who Thou art,
  Thou gentle, wondrous Boy."

Again His Voice falls on her ear,
  With melody divine;
"Teresa of Jesus is thy name,
  And—Jesus of Teresa, Mine!"

"Lord Jesus, to suffer and to be despised for Thy Sake."

Chapter Four

Saint John of the Cross

SAINT JOHN of the Cross, a man of exalted sanctity, called the "prince of mystic theology," was the chief co-laborer of Saint Teresa, in the establishment of the Reform, in Spain. He was an ardent lover of the Cross, and on one occasion, when Our Lord asked him what he desired as a reward for his labors and great austerity, he answered: "Lord to suffer, and to be despised for Thy Sake."

In the Office of his feast, which occurs on November 24, the Carmelites sing of Saint John of the Cross:

> "Saint of the eagle eye,
>   Gazing enrapt on high,
> Mid dread abysses of Divinity;
>   Martyr by heart's intent,
>   Virgin yet penitent;
> Prophet and guide in realms of mystery!
>   Clearly dost thou reveal
>   Secrets the clouds conceal,
> For thou hast steeped thy soul in rays above,
>   Pondering the mountain height,
>   Darkness of faith's long night,
> And the reviving flame of mystic love."

The fecundity of his luminous prose, and mystical writings, give proof of the Saint's ardent love for God. His writings rank high in literature, and the more outstanding of his works are: *Spiritual Canticle, The Ascent of Mount Carmel, The Living Flame of Love, The Dark Night, Precautions.*

Saint John of the Cross knew well how to "keep festival with the unleavened Bread of Sincerity and Truth" even in the midst of excruciating trials, imitating therein the meek Lamb of God in His bitter Passion. This valiant disciple of the Cross affords encouragement with this consoling truth: "When God is really loved, He hears most readily the cry of the soul that loves Him."

SAINT MARY MAGDALEN DI PAZZI

*The Seraphic Virgin of Carmel, Saint Mary **Magdalen** di Pazzi. "To suffer, not to die!"*

CHAPTER FIVE

Saint Mary Magdalen di Pazzi

THIS ILLUSTRIOUS Saint of Carmel was born on April 2, 1566, of the noble family of Camillo di Geri De-Pazzi, at Florence, Italy. When seventeen years of age, she entered the Carmelite Monastery of Saint Mary of the Angels, in Florence, taking the name of Sister Mary Magdalen.

During her entire religious life, she was favored with a series of ecstasies and raptures, during which she gave utterance to those wonderful maxims of Divine Love, and counsels of perfection, which were noted down by her companions at the time. Yet, these extraordinary favors in no way interfered with her usefulness, for she always performed her duties, and was most common-sense and efficient. When she became Mistress of Novices, she was divinely inspired to read their inmost thoughts, and God filled her with a wisdom to direct them aright.

Later when she was chosen to be Prioress of the Monastery, she governed the community with such love and charity, being consumed, as it were, with love of God, that the Sisters called her "Mother of Love." To her to love God meant "to suffer," and she really thirsted to suffer more and more, and prayed that her sufferings might be drawn out to the fullest extent. She hungered after Holy Communion.

Her seraphic sister, Saint Teresa of Avila, was guided by the motto: "To suffer, *or* to die," so, Saint Mary Magdalen di Pazzi directed hers in accordance with her own motto: "To suffer, *not* to die." No mere synopsis can give the faintest idea of the sanctity of her life, of the extent of her sufferings, or of her endless patience. Our Lord was pleased to try her in ways fearful and strange. Yet she was always obedient, observant of the Rule, humble and mortified, and she had a great reverence for the Religious life.

It will not be amiss to relate here a few of the marvelous favors accorded her during her life-time. On the occasion of her making a vow of virginity, Our Lord was pleased to present her with a precious ring. Whilst reciting the Divine Office in the choir, she often received the blessing of the Blessed Virgin Mary of Mount Carmel. Another time, kneeling in prayer, adoring the Blessed Sacrament, Our Lady placed in her arms the sweet Infant Jesus. As a reward for her steadfastness and holy purity, after countless trials and temptations, the Holy Mother of God placed upon her head a veil of dazzling whiteness. During one of her ecstasies, she had the ineffable joy to receive Holy Communion from Our dear Lord Himself. Our Blessed Lord permitted her to behold Saint Aloysius Gonzaga, the Jesuit, in the glory which he enjoys in Paradise. In joy she received a crown and a necklace of indescribable beauty; but she also received the sacred stigmata of the Lord Jesus. The great Doctor of the Church, Saint Augustine, engraved upon her heart these words: "Et Verbum caro factum est." (And the Word is made flesh.) Christ, her Divine Bridegroom placed a bridal ring upon her finger to symbolize the Mystical Nuptials.

Her saintly death was in accordance with her holy life, which occurred on May 25, 1607, in her forty-first year. She wrought many miracles even during her lifetime, and they were multiplied after her death. And now, after more than three centuries, the virginal body of Saint Mary Magdalen di Pazzi is still incorrupt, and lies in our Carmelite Monastery of the Ancient Observance, in Florence, Italy.

HYMN

In Honor of Saint Mary Magdalen di Pazzi

—1—

Seraph Saint of Carmel's Garden,
  Mystic child, of God, so fair;
Flower, blooming on Mount Carmel,
  Mary Magdalen, in prayer!

Chorus: Hearken, we pray,
      Seraph of Carmel!
      Hear our plea . . .
      On Carmel's way!

—2—

Hidden Saint, in holy silence,
  Scaling sure the Mountain's height;
Crosses made you smile more sweetly,
  Love for Jesus made them light.

Chorus: Hearken, etc.

—3—

Faithful child of Mother Mary,
  In thy arms reposed Her Child;
Clothed thee in Her pure, white mantle,
  Filled thy soul with graces mild.

Chorus: Hearken, etc.

36

—4—

Help us scale the Mount of Carmel,
  Keep us surely close to thee;
Lead us safe to Christ and Mary—
  To a blest Eternity!
Chorus: Hearken, etc.

"Oh, I would so love Him, love Him as He has never yet been loved! After my death I will let fall a shower of Roses! I will spend my Heaven in doing good upon earth."

CHAPTER SIX

Saint Therese of the Child Jesus

FROM THE once obscure Carmelite Monastery of Lisieux in France, comes the latest glory of Carmel, known throughout the world as the "Little Flower," "the white lily of Lisieux"—Saint Therese of the Child Jesus.

Known in the world as Therese Martin, she was born on January 2, 1873, in the little town of Alençon, of exemplary Catholic parents, the youngest of nine children. At fifteen years of age, she appealed to the Vicar of Christ, Pope Leo XIII, for permission to enter the austere Carmelite Order, in order to "pray for souls, but above all, to pray for Priests." Only nine short years she spent in the hallowed cloister of the Carmel of Lisieux, years bedewed with the spiritual lustre and exquisite fragrance of her sweetly angelic soul. They were years of quiet, unseen immolation; years of fruitful prayer, and of consuming love of God and souls.

Little Therese wished ardently to be a rose—a rose shedding its delicately pure petals on the road of God, through the world—on souls of sinners, and on hearts consecrated to Divine Love! And through the inexpressible mercy of God, she accomplished her mission—her glorious Carmelite mission: the sanctification of herself,

39

and the salvation of countless souls; souls of sinners, of Priests, of Religious, of people of every class.

But it was her life-goal, and no mere idle dream, to conquer the world for CHRIST. With this in mind, she scaled her Calvary, pouring forth her ceaseless prayers to God, so that she could truly say: "from the age of three, I have refused nothing to the good God." Read her exquisitely beautiful *Autobiography*, and learn the lessons expounded in so crystal-like clearness that you must imbibe therefrom a stimulating conception of the *interior life* of CARMEL—the Garden of MARY— so that flowers of every virtue, but especially the red rose of love, and the white rose of purity, may enhance, with marvelous effulgence, the garden of your soul.

You will wish to understand the reason why the Incomparable Mother of Carmel granted to Her "little Therese" the gracious vision of Her beautiful smile! So that you too, dear Reader, may help to fill the world with the "sweet odour" of Christ, with the variegated petals of a life lived according to the pattern given you by the Saints of CARMEL, live your life for God, in the world, in accordance with His Laws. Reflect the radiant beauty that scintillates from the Immaculate Heart of MARY, and diffuse everywhere the delicate fragrance of your purity, and the bright splendour of your truly Catholic living—so that all the world may know how sweet it is to love GOD.

Her Death—Beginning of Life

On that memorable evening of September 30, 1897, while the silver bells of the quiet Carmel sounded forth the evening Angelus, Sister Therese fixed her gaze of indescribable tenderness upon the Beautiful Flower of Carmel, MARY IMMACULATE, whose graceful statue enhanced her infirmary-cell. Silently, but full of hope, she gazed upon Mother Mary—STAR OF THE SEA! Lovingly, too, she pressed her little Crucifix to her love-filled heart—still trusting, still abandoning herself to HIM, in a complete oblation of soul and body.

And so, in a rapturous ecstacy of love, she died, as she had lived—of love! Her love-bruised heart could no longer bear the celestial torrents of God's love for her, nor the all-consuming fire of her love for God. Thus, He took her, this Little White Flower of Jesus, to Himself. The Divine Gardener transplanted His cherished "flower" to the fertile soil of the Carmel of Heaven—MARY'S GARDEN—where the Chaste Dove of the Heavenly Arc, the most resplendent Queen of Carmel, welcomed Her "Little Therese."

It is now many years since her soul, the enraptured soul of Saint Therese, has flown to the heights, and the astounding thing is that she continues her activity after death! Just to recall a few of her daring prophecies made during life, we note: "After my death, I will let

41

fall a shower of roses"; "I will spend my heaven, in doing good upon the earth"; "No one will invoke me without obtaining an answer!"

HER POWER WITH GOD

Daring "Little Therese" always admired the quaint "boldness" of Mary Magdalen, who dared to approach Our Lord in the house of the Pharisee, to anoint His Sacred Feet with precious ointment, and to wipe them dry with her beautiful golden hair. Little Therese's ineffable daring with the God of Love won for her a unique place in His Sacred Heart, and such power with God's Divine Heart, that Christ seemingly refuses her nothing.

Let us ask Saint Therese for her *Roses*. She kneels at the Feet of the fair Mother of Carmel, and this most sweet Mother is closest to the Blessed Trinity . . . Let us have confidence! May the ever-blooming "rose-flowers" of Saint Therese of Carmel, fall gently but surely upon the garden of our souls, and may their heavenly fragrance increase our love for JESUS and for MARY.

MIRACULOUS CRUCIFIX OF LUCCA

Replica of the Miraculous Crucifix of Lucca. Immense Crucifix towers over the Main Altar in the Monastery of Santa Croce di Lucca, in Naples, Italy.

CARMEL OF "SANTA CROCE DI LUCCA"

Carmelite Monastery of Santa Croce di Lucca.

CHAPTER SEVEN

The Old Vine

CARMEL IN NAPLES
1536.

THE ILLUSTRIOUS and saintly Father Nicholas Audet, General of the Carmelites for thirty-eight years, (1524-1562)—was instrumental in organizing a Monastery of Carmelite Nuns of the Ancient Observance, in the historic city of Naples, in Italy. Several members of the nobility of Naples, headed by the venerable Matrona Lucchese, who took the name of Sister Maria Cremona, established this first Neopolitan Carmel, in 1536-1537, under the title of the "Holy Cross of Lucca." The strict cloister was enjoined, together with the Holy Rule and Constitutions of the Carmelites of the Ancient Observance, in 1538, under the same General, the Most Reverend Father Nicholas Audet.

ITS TITLE

Carmel in Naples took its name in honor of the Holy Cross of Lucca (Santa Croce di Lucca), for the reason that the Monastery is in possession of a very large replica of the Miraculous Crucifix of Lucca. This immense Crucifix is placed over the Main Altar, in the Monastery (public) Chapel, for the veneration of the faithful.

There is a legend concerning this monastery, which tells us that Our Lord favored a poor musician, who played on his violin, before the Image on the original Crucifix, in Lucca. This poor musician was asking Our Lord for means to travel to the Holy Land. After he played, the Sacred Image stretched out one Foot, which was covered with a golden slipper, as if to invite him to take the precious shoe. The poor man was stunned at the "miracle" before his eyes, and hesitated even to touch the golden shoe. Finally, however, he accepted the offer, and went to a jeweler with his proffered gift. Having received the needed means for his pilgrimage, he departed on his way.

Meanwhile, the shoe was missed, and even traced to the jeweler's shop. It was brought back, but vain were the efforts made to try and replace the golden shoe. Our Lord hereby made it known that it was He Himself Who had given away the precious slipper.

Its Location

The Carmel of Naples stands on a hill half-way up the mountain called Vomero. And, as has been noted, the old Monastery is over four centuries old. The facts and events relating to the foundation of this ancient Monastery of the Calced Carmelites, in Naples, are still engraved on marble slabs and diligently preserved from generation to generation. The monastic rigor of the sacrificial cloistered life of prayer, with its unique simplicity, ardent fervour, and deep spirituality, continues in full vigor in the Carmel of Naples to this present day.

Its Offshoot—Carmel in the New World

We place special emphasis on the history of the Carmelite Monastery of Naples since it is from this most venerable and sweetly flourishing vine, that CARMEL of the ANCIENT OBSERVANCE has extended its verdant branches even across the placid waters of the Mediterranean Sea, stretching far past the wide ocean, giving to the New World a new GARDEN of CARMEL, under the heroic and zealous leadership of two distinguished daughters of Carmel: the Reverend Mother Therese of Jesus, and Sister Clement Mary of the Guardian Angel. Together these two able and courageous pioneers of Carmel founded the First Monastery of the CARMELITE NUNS of the ANCIENT OBSERVANCE, in the United States of America, choosing, with Ecclesiastical Approbation, *Saint Therese's Valley,* Lanark Manor, *ALLENTOWN, Pennsylvania,* as the appropriate site for the new CARMEL.

They dedicated their first American Calced Carmel to the Seraphic Virgin of the Calced Carmelites, SAINT MARY MAGDALEN DI PAZZI, and the Chapel to the world-famous "Little Flower," SAINT THERESE OF THE CHILD JESUS, under the protection of

THE QUEEN OF CARMEL, MARY

CONCEIVED WITHOUT SIN,

for the greater honor and glory of Her Divine Son,

OUR LORD, JESUS CHRIST!

PART II

Life of the First Foundress, Reverend Mother Therese of Jesus, Ord. Carm.

1877 - 1939

"Love watcheth, and sleeping slumbereth not. When weary it is not tired; when straitened it is not constrained when frightened is not disturbed; but like a vivid flame and a burning torch, it mounteth upwards, and securely passeth through all.

"Whosoever loveth knoweth the cry of this voice. A loud cry in the ears of God is that ardent affection of the soul which saith: 'O my God, my Love, Thou art all mine, and I am all Thine . . .' "

Imitation of Christ.

Some of Her Counsels

"God will provide!"

"Souls for Jesus and Mary through Saint Therese."

"Serve the Lord with joy!"

"Sacrifice is never to be laid aside."

"God loveth the cheerful giver!"

"We must learn to forget self."

"First and foremost, God's holy Will!"

"God fits the back for the burden."

'I would not miss Holy Communion for anything in the world!"

Mother Therese of Jesus, Ord. Carm.

Author's Note . . .

In order to comply with the pious requests on the part of our dear Sister-Carmels in the United States and abroad, and to satisfy the pressing entreaties of the ardent admirers of MOTHER THERESE OF JESUS, and the devoted friends of the CARMEL OF ALLENTOWN, we feel bound to give here an intimate description of the life of our lovable first Foundress, the Reverend Mother Therese of Jesus, so that souls may be strengthened by the example of the virtues practiced by Mother Therese.

May this humble history, like a living flame, be a light unto souls, and draw all hearts to run in the Way of Love, so that all may know how sweet it is to love and to serve God. And as the bright Star of Hope, our LADY OF LIGHT, attracts us to ascend, so too, may this brief story of the saintly "little Mother Therese," inspire all with a vehement longing to love and serve GOD faithfully; to extend the Reign of God's Love in every soul, to the utmost bounds of the earth, but especially in our dear America.

CHAPTER EIGHT

Mother Therese — Foundress

As our story unfolds, it will be readily understood that Mother Therese was indeed a very remarkable character and it is likewise true that once you met and spoke with her, you could not easily forget either her or the winning charm of her personality. She was in truth the soul of her Community. Beneath her modest reserve there was a simplicity and a gentleness of disposition that was evident in all she said or did. She knew how to be firm when the occasion demanded, but she was over-merciful rather than severe. Despite her mild temperament, she possessed a heart that was all on fire with zeal for God and her Order, so that she could truthfully say: "With zeal am I consumed for the Lord God of Hosts."

"Servite Domino in Laetitia."

Her expression was kindly and peaceful. It is said that the eyes are the windows of the soul and from out of the abundance of the heart the mouth speaketh! There was the sweetest reflections of peace in the eyes of Mother Therese and since she had learned to keep her interior in order from tender childhood, her deep spirituality could not but reveal itself even in her very countenance and she showed, unknowingly however, that her heart was immersed in Him Whom she loved above all. The refinement of her person, her extreme modesty, and the gentle dignity with which she treated persons and affairs, together with her extraordinary business capacities, gave her all that one would wish to find in a Foundress and an exemplary religious.

The purity of her gaze and the peacefulness which she constantly endeavored to maintain around her, gave a sweet and heavenly expression to her features, which were not beautiful but singularly attractive, so that one felt instinctively drawn to her. Her eyes were grey-blue, rather deep-set and penetrating, but clear and innocent as those of a child. They would sparkle merrily and light up with pleasure, and she could make her nuns laugh gayly too.

She liked her nuns to be always happy, always ready to smile, and if any one of them would sadden over some trifling occurrences, she would remind her sweetly: "No long faces, Sister. We cannot stand long faces." And it never took long for the culprit to be wreathed in smiles even though her cheeks were still wet with the dew of tears, because Mother Therese never hesitated to portray on her own dear countenance the picture of the "long face" before her.

Great was her delight when with her nuns in recreation, especially on some of the major feasts or on days when her anniversaries were celebrated. On these occasions the Sisters would prepare "surprises" and enact scenes, both pious and amusing, from the lives of the Saints. Mother Therese enjoyed these little festivities and entered into them with a simplicity and a joyfulness that delighted her spiritual children. Unfailingly she had a "surprise" for them too on such occasions, when she would herself prepare beforehand some little dainties or extra refreshments, different from the routine food, so that these happy events were sought after and eagerly looked forward to by all with child-like anticipation.

Mother and Prioress

An exemplary Prioress, she was a real Mother in the highest and dearest sense of the term. She rejoiced with the joyful and she knew how to comfort and to sympathize with those in affliction. Loaded down with the multiplicity of her important and ever-increasing duties, she would lay aside everything in order to pour upon some saddened heart words of cheer and solace. Always bearing in mind that her first duty was to her nuns, she looked after everyone in such a manner that each Sister thought herself the special object of her maternal solicitude.

Even during the night-hours, it happened not infrequently, that one of the Sisters, thinking it was time for rising and not seeing the light under the cell-door of the Prioress, rapped at her cell and called Mother Therese out of bed. It was only after Mother Therese was fully dressed and had ventured downstairs, that the large clock showed her the Sister's mistake and that it was hours before the actual rising time. When morning dawned at last, no word of reproach rose to Mother Therese's lips, nor did she herself ever mention the matter to anyone. She acted in the same manner when the nuns would disturb her during her hours of rest, to seek medicinal relief for various ills.

She did not like to see uncalled-for tears particularly when they bore the unmistakable sign of self-pity. She wanted her nuns to be courageous and would often remind them of their glorious title of "Sisters of the Blessed Virgin Mary of Mount Carmel." And she would admonish them firmly with "let us live up to our sublime title." One of the nuns had the tendency to shed tears every once in a while; in fact, this was her usual custom when things went contrary. Mother Therese prudently commenced to check this weakness from the very beginning and so presented her spiritual daughter with a holy card and in her own hand wrote an appropriate poem on the reverse side, starting out with: "To my dear little child 'Dribble-drop' . . . " The title itself so amused the good Sister that from thenceforth, she strove diligently and successfully to overcome her weakness.

Another Sister felt great timidity when it came her turn to chant alone in the middle of the Choir and it was customary for her to give evidence to many a "downpour of pearls." When the great Feast of Christmas came around, the observant Mother had a package for this Sister, and addressing her by a new name, wrote: "To my dear little 'Dolorosa of the Sorrowful Countenance' . . . " It had the desired effect.

Mother Therese recognized the fact that no two souls are alike, so she dealt with her nuns accordingly. But all could well affirm that with her it was the easy approach of a child to its Mother. Such filial love and confidence did she inspire in the hearts of her spiritual daughters that each one strove generously and unceasingly to make her heavy tasks less burdensome. She was their living exemplar and it was her heroic energy in the service of Our Lord and her wonderful desire to accomplish great things for God and for souls, that stimulated her nuns to undertake the actual building of the beautiful Carmel which now graces "Saint Therese's Valley."

"In the second year of my novitiate," relates one of the nuns, "I was confined to our cell on account of illness. Our dear Reverend Mother Therese, as was her wont with us all, could hardly do enough to make me comfortable. Toward evening the weather became cool.

Ever on the alert, she stood beside our bed, a warm blanket in her dear hands and gently laid it over me. I was deeply moved. I recognized that blanket. She had removed it from her own bed. 'What a lesson for me,' I thought, 'to deny oneself in order to accommodate another!' Indeed my own dear Mother could not have done more for me than had our dear Mother Therese."

On her feast-day, October 15, 1934, the festal celebrations, as was the custom on such occasions, were opened with the recitation of a poem addressed to her and deftly penned by one of the nuns. The underlying thought contained in the little verses reveals the child-like love and esteem they had for their venerable Foundress:

CHERISHED MOTHER

How full our hearts, for you, in tenderness,
    Long to express their wishes, joy to bring,
And light your Mother-heart! May Jesus bless
    Your happy day, we softly sing!

Full well you know why we, in love, unveil
    Our present song, in notes of youthful bliss;
Such happy day, Your Feast, omits travail:
    Mere words cannot reveal the depth of this.

May Jesus on thy virgin-heart unfold
    His pure caress, in loving accents rare.
What greater plea can offer Love? Untold
    Thy love for Him, so sweet, O Mother fair!

HER GENEROSITY

How beautifully true it is that the highest token of love is to give one's life for one's friend. Even Saint Therese, the Little Flower of Jesus, was most deeply impressed with these words which came from Eternal Truth Himself. And in her sweet canticle, "I Thirst For Love," she writes:

"In wondrous love Thou didst come down from Heaven
>To immolate Thyself O Christ for me,—
So in my turn, my love to Thee is given
>I wish to suffer and to die for Thee!
Thou, Lord, hast spoken this truth benign . . .
>'To die for one loved tenderly
>Of greatest love on earth is sign'
And now, such love is mine—
>Such love for Thee!"

Well, Mother Therese did this very thing! She loved her Spouse most tenderly . . . Her deeds prove that. She lived, she died for Him. She had given Him everything, yes, life itself.

God was her Changeless Friend. Frequently she would say: "God Alone suffices; God never changes." And she was changeless in her love of Him. Trials would come and almost unbearable crosses; thorns, too, whose sharpness would have depressed a less valiant soul than hers; even the necessity of scaling Calvary—all this was her portion. In fact, we are forced to admit that in the course of her long career, innumerable were the crosses laid on the holy Foundress, but some of them are too intimate and too bitter to be revealed here below. However, God's grace, like refreshing dew to a little flower, came down upon her soul, in torrents.

Mother Therese, just about medium height, looked smaller than she really was, especially in the last years of her life when her shoulders seemed bent beneath the many burdens of her great undertaking. Her powers of endurance were very great and no one will ever know the secret martyrdom she underwent owing to ill health. She was not given to speaking of her aches and pains, and never did ill health prove an obstacle to any of her work. Towards the end of her life, when her heart-attacks became a little more frequent, and her gentle countenance paled more and more, her nuns dreaded what actually took place on the morning of April 11th, 1939, the day of Mother Therese's death.

"God fits the back for the burden," Mother Therese would fondly declare both by speech and in the countless letters she had to write, which letters kept her sitting at her desk till way into the night. Truly wonderful it was how she managed to fulfill her busy days, week after week, month after month. She was on the go constantly, interviewing business men, the different contractors and builders; overseeing the workmen and the work being done; looking after each and every detail of the building no matter how trifling, with a keenness of mind and an

58

enthusiasm of energy that only God could have inspired. Then too, she looked after and attended the spiritual exercises of her community with the same exactness and fervor as always. This spirit was heightened by grace as is revealed in the beautiful incidents that took place on the last few days prior to her death and which we will treat of in another chapter.

HER CHARITY

We do not exaggerate when we say that she practiced the golden virtue of charity in an eminent degree. Enduring bodily pain herself for so many years, she was quick to observe the little ills and pains of everybody else and would go herself to seek a soothing remedy for others, never stopping to think of her own fatigues nor the multiplicity of her ever-increasing duties. Then with her usual smile and a few encouraging words, she solaced their bodily as well as their spiritual infirmities. Should the occasion prove an appropriate one, she would even remind them of Purgatory, and that it was far better to suffer a little here than to make expiation in the next life.

As has been said, all the nuns without exception found her easy of approach when seeking corporal relief or spiritual solace. A little incident typical of this occurred a day or so before her death. One of the nuns showed signs of weakness while at work; this did not escape the notice of Mother Therese, who presented the nun with a tiny glass of wine. Looking at the pale, care-worn face of her beloved Prioress, the nun hesitated to take the medicinal relief, saying: "Mother, won't you take it instead? You need it more than I."

Sacrifice was a most sweet food to her. She chose to escape all unnecessary alleviations; she was not eager to seek relief from pain. But with her spiritual daughters, she outdid herself to grant them every comfort whether temporal or spiritual.

Her charity extended far beyond the walls of her dear Carmel. On the very evening before her death, although suffering with acute pains in her chest, she went from room to room in the offices, in search of an appropriate gift for a poor young man who had assisted at the carpentry work in the new building. She herself arranged the gift in a small box together with a Rosary to present to the poor boy.

Meanwhile the heart of her faithful assistant, Mother Clement Mary, was growing very sad. She, as the constant companion of Mother Therese, was keenly aware, more than anyone else in the community, that the venerable Mother's failing health could not endure much longer under the awful pressure of her work. Often did she plead with Mother to take some relaxation, but her entreaties went unheeded. God's loving Providence had enabled Mother Therese to make great strides in the work assigned to her, and if He wished her to complete the vast undertaking, He would certainly proportion His grace to the work and give her the strength and health necessary to carry on. Should health fail her, well . . . , He was free to accomplish His holy Will in her regard!

Unless we forget this body of ours we will never make any progress in perfection—wrote the great mystic of Carmel, Saint Teresa of Avila. And Mother Therese lived according to the maxim that "we must forget self." And, like her fond Patroness, she never preached anything that she did not first practice herself.

Her marvelous trust in God's Providence that "GOD WILL PROVIDE" (which was constantly on her lips), brought many a frown of disapproval from some of the Superiors who naturally preferred that her material backing, in view of so great a building project, would be a little more visible and secure.

God has His own way of bringing about the accomplishment of His designs. On one occasion, in face of opposition, she had responded very gently as was her custom, saying: "Well, it is not surprising that we have to encounter obstacles of every kind. I share the same lot in this as did the holy Mother Saint Teresa." "What," she was asked, "do you compare yourself to the great Saint Teresa?" The humble Mother was not in the least disturbed by the inquiry which was intended to humiliate her. In fact, she possessed an amazing fund of wit and therefore would more likely try to see the bright side of any dark situation. Although amused at the outbreak, she made no response. She smiled.

HER GRATITUDE

Among her many beautiful characteristics was gratitude; this lovely virtue Mother Therese exemplified to a very eminent degree. In the first years of the Allentown foundation, many friends assisted Mother Therese and her noble work, both monetarily and by giving their time and free service. With the passing of the years, however, and change of circumstances, many were unable to continue their cheerful generosity. Others again simply grew indifferent after awhile. But it must be said that the greater number of these "first friends" remained always faithful and sincere. In regard to those who grew indifferent, we recall the following incident.

Christmas time came around. Mother Therese, with a group of nuns, was busily engaged in preparing special gift-tokens for the benefactors. One of the Sisters ventured to cross out from the list the names of all those who showed little or no interest in the Carmel. Mother Therese stopped her immediately and declared, "They have helped us in the past and *we must always be grateful for what they have done.*"

Such gratitude on her part broke down many barriers of indifference. Writing to one of the early benefactors some years after he had taken up residence in another state, Mother Therese ended her letter in the following manner: "Assuring you, dear friend, of our humble but fervent prayers, and thanking you, once more, for all you have done for us . . ." Her sincere expression of unfailing gratitude merited a beautiful response from this good friend, who replied: "Your letters always impress me and I marvel at your gratitude and how you never fail, dear Mother, to thank me for the little I did for your beautiful work. I only wish I could come back and do a whole lot more." (This extract was taken from a letter written by Rev. Brother Stanislaus Reybitz, Ord. Carm.)

Again, her spirit of gratitude was magnificently portrayed when she spoke of her own dear mother toward whom she cherished a most tender love and affection. She would counsel her nuns to be grateful to God for the gift of exemplary parents, who had raised them in the true Faith, and from babyhood on, had taught and trained them in all that was good and pure. Her own father had died when she was about three years of age, so it is natural that all her life she kept referring to her pious mother whom God called to Himself when Mother Therese was barely thirteen years of age.

CHAPTER NINE

Early Years of Mother Therese

MOTHER THERESE, known in the world as Anna Marie Lindenberg, was born of Joseph and Marianna Lindenberg, in Muenster, Westphalia, on May 20, 1877, the youngest of four children. Four days later, on May 24, she was brought to the Cathedral of Muenster for baptism.

A victim of the dread disease cancer, Mrs. Lindenberg had but one desire she wished fulfilled before her death and prayed earnestly that Our Lord would see fit to grant it. She nourished the hope that little Anna Marie might have her First Holy Communion advanced a year because her mother felt death approaching and yearned for this consolation. She felt urged to take the matter up with the pastor. It looked rather hopeless but she prayed on, and her request was granted, for Anna Marie was permitted to receive Holy Communion on April 13, 1890. She was well prepared for the great event, and it was indeed with a fond Mother's pride that Mrs. Lindenberg arrayed her little one in the lily-white dress and veil in which she was to be, for the first time, the little bride of Jesus.

Years later, when she recounted this memorable occasion, Mother Therese's eyes shone with a wistful light
and there were tears of joy and of gratitude when she
remembered her pain-stricken mother whose last act on
earth was to prepare the heart of her youngest child for
the first reception of Jesus.

From this good mother, indeed, little Anna Marie,
who was destined by the Almighty to become a nun, and
a foundress of a Carmel, surely must have gleaned her
marvelous spirit of self-sacrifice. She seemed always to
be permeated, as it were, with the fact that "God sees
it" and that sufficed for her.

She loved to remind her nuns that she had been born
on Pentecost Sunday. At birth she was so very weak, so
very small, almost too frail to give hope of any future
career. To save the failing infant, the doctors prescribed
goats' milk on which the little one throve and waxed
strong.

Her Childhood

When about four or five years of age, little Anna
Marie and her group of playmates were interrupted at
play by a Gypsy troupe which was passing by in a
strange-looking wagon. The children were attracted to
the wagon by some toys and playthings that happened to
catch their eyes and approaching nearer were cordially
received by the Gypsies and invited to play with the

toys. As soon as the last child entered, the wagon sped away out of the town. In a neighboring city, the wagon stopped for a few moments before a hotel at which point little Anna Marie caught sight of a familiar figure, and recognized her elder brother Henry. "Heinrich, Heinrich," she called pleadingly, and the young man, amazed to find at last that the familiar little voice of his own sister came from the strange-looking wagon, approached the van hastily and was about to snatch little Anna Marie away when one of the Gypsies, with knife in hand, slashed him across the face. Nevertheless Henry held on to his little charge and with face bleeding, safely rescued his little sister from the would-be kidnappers.

A more amusing incident in her life took place when, with some of her little companions, she delighted in playing at being "a Sister"; and, at other times, she, with one particular chum, would run off to the woods and play at being "a hermit." Once, when she and her little friends were garbed as "Sisters," they decided to "build their convent" alongside the theatrical house. No sooner had the "holy nuns" pitched their tent when a group of players alighted from the theatre for a stroll on the grounds. The players were dressed in worldly fashion. The "little Sisters," who had been rigidly instructed in modesty of dress, became actively zealous, and approached the group, calling to them in a loud voice: "Vanity, vanity, and all is vanity."

The Divine Seal

Anna Marie loved Sundays when she went with her mother to the Capuchin Monastery in Muenster to assist at the Holy Sacrifice of the Mass. This was her greatest delight!

At eight years of age, she accompanied her mother to the Convent of the Sisters of Our Lady of Charity. Here she witnessed her cousin's reception into the Congregation of the Good Shepherd Sisters. The Clothing Ceremony made a deep impression on the little girl and from that moment she conceived an ardent desire to give herself as a consecrated bride to the Saviour.

Little did the innocent child realize that long years would pass before she would see the fulfillment of her young heart's cherished desire. But time and travail only served to strengthen her resolution of soul, and never for a moment did she depart from her determination to give herself wholly to Jesus. The seed was planted and it would require the Divine Gardener Himself to bring to flower that precious vocation, which sorely needed the life-giving rays of an effulgent Sun for its transplanting to the Mystical Garden of Carmel.

School Years

Anna Marie was an excellent pupil. Even at an early age, she possessed an extraordinary skill for memorizing.

68

And we would like to mention here that after fifty years or more, she could recite with ease a very long poem which she had been called upon to deliver before the Emperor of Germany upon his visit to her childhood school.

Although younger in years, Anna Marie excelled her companions in almost every subject, but she ranked highest in mathematics and proved an expert with the needle. These two remarkable natural talents would be most valuable assets to her and presaged her subsequent outstanding executive ability. To her school mistress, she owed her first lessons in meditation. This worthy teacher, marked by a fixed exterior rigidity, possessed nevertheless a sterling character and deep spirituality. She it was who taught her apt pupil the art of meditating and how to fix her thoughts and heart upon God so as to commune with Him interiorly. These "first lessons" left a lasting impression on the young contemplative, who never forgot the precious instructions nor the dear teacher who was so worthy of her noble profession.

The good God was laying a deep bed in the soul of Anna Marie and He prepared her well, as is His wont. Later events proved, without doubt, that Our Lord was pleased to lay a solid foundation in the spiritual up-bringing of His future spouse.

Chapter Ten

Her Fidelity

As has been mentioned, Anna Marie was barely thirteen years old when God called her beloved mother to Himself. She had always been a sweet consolation to her dear mother and now especially, in the last hours as her mother lingered on, she was a heavenly solace to her and never left her side. All through the dreary night Anna Marie watched and prayed beside her mother, her one desire being to give all she could to the mother who was about to leave her, and whom she loved most on earth.

Thus we see that even in the very flower of her girlhood, the saintly Mother Therese practiced self-forgetfulness and loyal perseverance. No wonder that in later years, she would with seeming ease, deny herself the necessary sleep and rest that should have been hers. When business or charity prevented her from taking her meals at the proper time, she would go without them completely, so as not to cause any extra work for any of her nuns.

After her dear Mother's death, Anna Marie wanted no outside help in the things that had to be done because they were the last she could do before the body of her cherished parent would be laid away forever.

She herself took complete charge of the funeral arrangements; looked after everything and faced the situation with a foresight and a courage that was far beyond her years. Well could she say, however, as did the Virgin of Lisieux, Saint Therese of the Child Jesus, that her path, from the very outset, was strewn with thorns rather than with roses.

Henceforward, difficulties, one after the other, were to confront her; however, she had by this time mastered the art of total dependence on God so that no obstacle proved too great for her. She faced all obstacles and took hold of every situation with an adaptability that was simply second nature to her.

> "The Lord is my shepherd; how can
> I lack anything?" (Ps. 22.)

At this period of her life, Anna Marie felt that it was the proper time to make known to her legal guardian her desire to become a religious. Her disclosure met with an unsympathetic response and instant refusal, and there was no change of attitude to be hoped for before she would reach her twenty-first year. God's loving Providence would not abandon His trusting child for whom He had special designs.

Anna Marie maintained a filial correspondence with her uncle, her mother's brother, the Reverend Albert M. Horck, S.J., who had come to America many years before and was a pastor in Saint Louis, Missouri. Gentle and refined by nature, endowed with a deep spirituality, Father Horck filled his letters with wise and prudent counsels. It was through the influence of this zealous missionary that Anna Marie made preparations to leave her Fatherland and come to America.

Anna Marie had little natural desire to leave her native soil, her friends, and relatives, and all the memories of the years passed in her native town. However, trained from earliest years in obedience, she felt that her Priest-uncle's advice was to be obeyed. So, with the beautiful simplicity which was always so characteristic of her, Anna Marie accomplished her sacrifice.

After her arrival in the United States, she lost no time in learning the English language, and, remarkable to relate, in a very short time, she could write and speak it fluently. Trained in fine music and organ, Anna Marie was installed as organist in the parish church, and was also charged with the direction of the choir. Endowed with good health, she found joy in manual labor. She took care of the household. An expert in home-economics, she was simply nonpareil in maintaining the household, and in the art of cooking. Circumstances unfailingly proved how gifted she was with great common sense.

Reverend Father Horck was fully aware of his niece's ardent desire for the deep, interior life of the cloister. He promised to help her, but on account of his rapidly-declining health, he was compelled at this time to transfer to Verboort, in Oregon. This change of plans meant a fresh sacrifice for Anna Marie, whose courage and determination were put to additional test. However, in the same spirit as her own dear mother had practiced the virtue of self-sacrifice, so too, this valiant soul, thirsting ardently for the waters of a deeper spiritual life, away from the world, was willing to sacrifice longing for duty. For such she deemed it, a sacred duty to care for this aged missionary whose days were now numbered and whose health was utterly spent after many years of faithful service in the vineyard of the Lord.

"All my life thy loving favour pursues me; through the long years, the Lord's house shall be my dwelling-place." (Ps. 22, 6.)

It is next to impossible to describe the pain of longing when Our Divine Lord is the tender Object of such ardent desire. God's watchful Providence continued to exercise vigilance over this privileged soul whose yearning to fly to her Beloved, would, in His own good time, be realized; when at last, she would bid adieu to the world in which she had gone about doing good.

Our Lord soon showed His faithful servant the special designs He had in bringing her to Verboort. Here she met the saintly and venerable priest, the Reverend Father H. J. McDevitt, D.D., former Rector of the North American College in Rome, Italy. Destined by

74

the Almighty, Reverend Father McDevitt, distinguished for his zeal as well as for his learning, was to play a very important role in the life of this heroic child. His devoted and paternal guidance would prove a significant factor in her spiritual destiny.

About this time also, Anna Marie had the good fortune to have as her soul's director, an eminent ascetic, in the person of the Reverend Father Henry A. Gabriel, S.J., who according to the wise decree of Providence, was to exercise a special influence on her inner life. Hence, her prolonged delay in the world was not without its recompense from Him for Whom she so lovingly and so submissively bore this heavy trial. On May 26, 1912, Our Lord was pleased to call to Himself the soul of her dear uncle, Father Albert M. Horck, at Saint Mary's in Oregon.

Chapter Eleven

A Long Pilgrimage

It was some time after this that Anna Marie, upon the advice of her venerable director, Reverend Father Mc-Devitt made plans for a pilgrimage to Lourdes, France, to seek the guidance of Our Lady, her Star of Hope, and to visit the Marian Shrines in Italy. The prospective tour was to be made in company with her intimate friend, Marguerite M. of Athens, Wisconsin.

Fortunately we have on hand letters and notes of the future Mother Therese, wherein she very aptly describes her memorable pilgrimage, and so, we feel privileged to give here, her personal account.

At Lourdes

" . . . On May 13 we arrived at Bordeaux where we visited a few of the more ancient Churches. From here we journeyed to Lourdes. Arrived at Lourdes, what happiness I felt to kneel at the Feet of the Immaculate Conception, where the poor shepherd girl, Bernadette, was destined to receive so many heavenly visitations. Here indeed I myself was deeply impressed by the near-ness of the Queen of Heaven, that I felt urged to cry out with the Apostle, 'Lord, it is good to be here.' And so I remained at the Grotto, sleepless, until about midnight.

"About four o'clock on the following morning, I went back to the Grotto. No wonder that little Bernadette felt such an intense attraction for this blessed spot. And behold, on my arrival at the Grotto, I found other pilgrims who had preceded me thereto, and a Priest had commenced to offer the Holy Sacrifice of the Mass. During this Mass, I had the happiness to receive Our Lord in Holy Communion.

"Here too, I could present to the Mother of Grace, all my intentions. And not being able to tear myself away, I remained at the Grotto to assist at a number of holy Masses.

"How pathetic it was to behold the sick and the infirm pleading with the Heavenly Queen, with child-like trust and edifying fervour, for the favour of cure, of resignation, of restoration of health . . .

"There are three beautiful Churches erected on this hallowed place, wherein, also, I had the privilege to assist at a number of Masses. Later on, I visited the poor "home" of Bernadette, saw the miserable furnishings, her pitiable bed, and other items which served the child of grace. To me it seemed as though the message of Our Lady could be applied right here: 'Because He hath regarded the humility of His handmaid; for behold from henceforth all generations shall call me blessed. For He that is mighty hath done great things for me: and holy is His Name. And His mercy is from generation to generation: unto them that fear Him . . .'

"Much, and very much has little Bernadette endured and now she is exalted so highly in Heaven. Yes, God is marvelous in His Saints.

"In the evening, there was the singularly impressive candlelight procession, and from a thousand lips and hearts you could hear the exquisitely touching refrain: 'Ave, Ave Maria' . . . "

In Rome

From Lourdes, Anna Marie and her companion journeyed to Rome, arriving in the Eternal City on a Sunday morning. Space does not permit us to print all the notes and letters of Mother Therese, which are always so edifying, and a delicate diffusion of the loveliness of her own soul's deep spiritualization. She wrote: "It would take too long to give a complete description of our pilgrimage . . ." Quite simply and with charming candor of expression, she goes on to describe the impressions she received when assisting at the various ceremonies in Saint Peter's. Likewise, on three different occasions, the future Carmelite foundress had the privilege of an audience with the Holy Father.

She was overjoyed and truly happy over her experiences both at Lourdes, and in Rome, where she and her companion visited all the sanctuaries of note.

"I was vividly impressed," she continues, "by my visit to the Coliseum, and to the arena where so many martyrs shed their blood for the Faith. Afterwards we visited the Mamertine Prison, and saw the column to which Saint Peter had been chained. We also drank from the well in the prison which is said to have appeared miraculously after Saint Peter's prayer to God for water with which to baptize his fellow-prisoners.

"We visited the Catacombs, the room in which Saint Cecilia was martyred, as also the beautfiul Church, dedicated in her honor.

"I had the happiness to receive hospitality, for three days, in the paternal home of Saint Agnes, alongside of which is the Church, bearing her name, and in which her precious relics are carefully preserved. I walked leisurely through the rose - garden, where the virgin - saint had played as a child, and where she so frequently communed with God. All of this evoked in my memory, vivid scenes from the story of Fabiola.

"Upon concluding our visits throughout Rome, we travelled to Naples, where we attended an impressive Corpus Christi procession. In fact, it seemed that the whole town turned out for the solemn affair. In the afternoon, we venerated the relics of Saint Januarius,

80

and thence went on to the ancient Monastery of San Martino, located on the highest peak of the Vomero, from which altitude one may behold a panoramic view of the entire surroundings, but especially, of the picturesque Bay of Naples.

"We visited the Isle of Capri, the city of Venice, and thence, went on to Padua, a city acolor with decorations, and alive with festivity, on account of the feast of Saint Anthony. Over a thousand pilgrims venerated the incorrupt relic of the Saint.

"From here, we went on to Assisi, to the venerable old Church of Our Lady of Angels, the "Portiuncula," the cradle of the Franciscan Order. We viewed the "miraculous" rose-bushes, into which Saint Francis threw himself, during a time of temptation. Since that occasion, the roses on these bushes are without thorns.

"We had the pleasure to view the relics and souvenirs of Saint Clare.

"Our next stop was in Florence, where we visited the old Monastery of Saint Mary Magdalen di Pazzi, and I was delighted to receive from the Reverend Mother Prioress, a precious relic of this glorious Saint of Carmel's Old Observance

"In Milan, we admired the great work of art, the beautiful Cathedral, in which is preserved the relic of an illustrious Cardinal, Saint Charles Borromeo. Also, in one of the side Chapels, may be found a magnificent painting of Da Vinci's "LAST SUPPER," with which we were deeply impressed."

"Lead Thou Me On ..."

As has been said, it was in obedience to her spiritual Guide, the Reverend Father McDevitt, who, aware of the integrity of her valiant character, had encouraged her steps in this direction, with the hope that this perse-vering child of the Saviour, would be better able to discern the Divine Will, in regard to her soul.

But, alas, she would continue to drink deeply from the chalice of disappointment. The pierced Hand of her Divine Spouse was lavish in His bestowal of the cross throughout her whole life, but not for one moment did her trust in Him waver. No wonder, then, that later on in her dear Monastery at Allentown, she would very, very often repeat to her spiritual daughters: "God fits the back for the burden."

CHAPTER TWELVE

Vocation to Carmel

Now THAT Anna Marie's obligations were over, she was free to follow the call of the Divine Master after long years of patient, heroic waiting. It was the zealous Father Gabriel, S.J., who directed her steps to the ark of sacred Carmel which she entered on the Feast of Saint Teresa of Avila, October 15, 1913, taking the name of Sister Therese of Jesus.

The Reverend Mother of the Carmel, herself a humble soul, distinguished for unalterable meekness and kindness, before long recognized in her new daughter, Sister Therese, a soul of solid virtue and singular holiness. Thus, under the personal guidance of this worthy Prioress and true spiritual Mother, Sister Therese of Jesus commenced a new era of increased fervour, of interior peace, and of greater joy in God's service.

On May 6, 1914, the Feast of Saint John before the Latin Gate, she had the ineffable joy of receiving the Holy Habit of Carmel from the Bishop of the diocese. About a year later, on July 16, 1915, the Feast of the Incomparable Patroness of the Order, Our Lady of

Mount Carmel, Sister Therese of Jesus was permitted to pronounce her Holy Vows.

In this connection, she wrote to her intimate friend on September 20, 1916

" . . . I had the great grace of receiving the Holy Habit of Carmel on the 6th of May 1914, the feast of the beloved disciple Saint John, commemorating on that day his martyrdom—his being plunged into boiling oil. And this ardent lover of the Crucified, whom from that day on I considered as my special protector, obtained for me the privilege of making my Profession and pronouncing my Final Vows, which bind me forever to Jesus Crucified, on the Feast of Our Lady of Mount Carmel, July 16, 1915. Yes, indeed, I feel that Our Lord was addressing me in a similar manner: 'Behold thy Mother.' And surely, *Mary* has been truly my good dear Mother from that day on *in a special manner*. Nothing more is wanting to me now but to bind myself closer and closer to Him Who is the sole object of all my thoughts and affections. In this sacred union I find all the desires of my heart fulfilled. All else I find utterly useless and insipid."

Even after the great day of her religious Profession, Sister Therese of Jesus continued to apply herself unceasingly to the work of her sanctification, happy and contented in her humble, hidden life.

In addition to her extraordinary spiritual assets, Sister Therese of Jesus possessed, as has been hinted at heretofore, great practical abilities and great talents. She was chosen to write letters for the aged Prioress who appreciated her facile, refined style of composition and her edifying message of gratitude to the benefactors of the Monastery. Excelling in choir work, Sister Therese performed each and every duty in a most admirable manner. No matter to what task she was assigned, be it ever so lowly or otherwise, whether in the kitchen, laundry, or at housework, she was ever most reliable and fulfilled even the smallest duty with a perfection that seemed second nature to her.

The venerable Prioress regarded her as a treasure, and when the Prioress became bedfast, about two years prior to her death, the saintly old Mother appointed Sister Therese of Jesus to be Infirmarian. Sister Therese, she well knew, was remarkable for sweetness of disposition, and indeed fraternal charity had impressed its beautiful seal upon her soul long before she entered the portals of her dear Carmel.

God called the venerable Mother to her Eternal Reward. Previous to this she had cast a look of affectionate gratitude upon her devoted Infirmarian and said to her, most prophetically, as if peering into the future: "You poor child!" But it was only the beginning of new trials for this true daughter of Carmel, who humbly acquiesced to the Divine Will and continued her trust in the Saviour. Her simplicity of heart and her deep, abiding faith did not allow her to be guided by mere sentiment at any time.

Ten years of close intimacy with the Master, in the silence of the cloister, had sped rapidly by.

CHAPTER THIRTEEN

Carmel in Europe

*"O the depths of the riches of the wisdom and of
the knowledge of God! How incomprehensible
are His judgments, and how unsearchable
His ways!" (Rom. XI.)*

EVER SINCE her memorable pilgrimage to Italy, Sister
Therese of Jesus maintained a friendly correspondence
with the Carmelites of Holland, and of Freiburg. At
that time, the latter were forming a new community and
so were very much in need of material help. Sister
Therese had, at the time, assisted them most generously
with the aid of some of her friends to the extent that
the Sisters managed to purchase a house and land for a
suitable Monastery. It may be noted here that, years
later, this same Convent was taken over by the nuns
from the Monastery of Dueren, and today is a very
flourishing Carmel. The Sisters at Freiburg never forgot
their kind benefactress. Strangely enough, it was to
their nascent community that Sister Therese of Jesus,
with the proper Apostolic authority, was transferred,
and where she was to do the work of a "foundress."

A painful trial was connected with this incident in her life. She bore it valiantly. Indeed for a soul of ordinary spirituality such a cross would have been a most severe trial. But God knows His "timber," and as He seemingly smote with one Hand, so with the other He upheld His faithful spouse and strengthened her with the Divine Seal of the Cross.

Sister Therese of Jesus took over her new duties at that Carmel with the same devotedness and care that she had always manifested. Here, it seems, her special work was to foster vocations by means of correspondence. Gifted with the pen and conversant with several languages, it seems that she was charged particularly with the handling of American correspondence.

Outwardly all went well. But we must not suppose that matters arranged themselves smoothly for God's faithful "mendicant" whose new title of "Mother" only added fresh responsibilities and increased cares, plus the burden of helping with the direction of souls. Concomitantly with His yoke, here at Freiburg, Mother Therese's courage and equanimity were put to many a hard test and trying circumstance, most of which history need not go down in print. Let it suffice that all is inscribed in the book of eternity!

> "O magnify the Lord with me; and let us
> extol His Name together." (Ps. 33, 4.)

The Almighty, Who directs all things, inspired Marie Elizabeth Roessler, of Belfield, North Dakota, to seek admission, at this time, into the Carmel of Porta Coeli, in Wuerzburg, Bavaria, where her aunt and cousin were, for many years, members of that fervent community. Their quota being completed at the time, her petition was forwarded to the Sisters at Freiburg, where it was received by Mother Therese of Jesus, who, as noted heretofore, was made responsible for American correspondence.

Encouraged by the gracious and edifying communications of Mother Therese, Marie Elizabeth left American shores and embarked for Europe, with the intention of joining the community at Freiburg.

In this manner, Divine Providence sent to the intrepid Mother Therese her first spiritual daughter, the future Sister Clement Mary of the Guardian Angel. And, indeed, to the very end, she would prove a veritable "guardian angel" to the beloved Foundress, both of whom would accomplish God's holy Will, although their life-work was not destined to flower on foreign soil.

> "The joy of my life consists in my intimacy
> with the Guest Who resides within my soul."
> (Sister Elizabeth of the Trinity)
> Carmel of Dijon.

As things were at Freiburg, it seemed that no immediate steps would be taken to make it a monastery of strict enclosure. But what weighed on Mother Therese more heavily was the responsibility she had assumed to have encouraged the young Marie Elizabeth's long ocean voyage, for the purpose of entering a community that did not promise positively a Garden Enclosed for the glory of the Blessed Virgin Mary of Mount Carmel and Her Divine Son. But then she reminded herself that all was in the Hands of the Divine Gardener Who had arranged for the transplanting. She was merely His poor handmaid . . .

Persevering soul that she was, Mother Therese lost none of her confidence in the God of Love. Indeed, trials, sufferings of body and soul, augmented her blind trust and her immutable hope in the good God. Nevertheless her heart was not entirely at rest, and she felt that, in her new mission, she was not giving herself completely to her Divine Spouse. In order that her contemplative soul might find that "cleft in the rock" which she earnestly longed for, she wrote to her friend, the Mother Abbess of the Trappistines, at "Maria Altbronn" in Alsace-Lorraine, revealing her inmost sentiments and confiding to her the secret yearnings of her soul. Like the holy Cure d' Ars, Mother Therese was tempted to reach out for the solitude and silence of La Trappe.

But man proposes and God disposes! He it was Who wished this choice flower to bloom in no other but in MARY'S Garden of CARMEL, so redolent of a hidden spiritual beauty, the sweet fruit of trial borne patiently and lovingly, like the flowers of the field, submissive to sun and rain, under the watchful Eye of the Divine Gardener Who seemingly desired to prune and to prune, whilst with the left Hand, He upheld and tenderly embraced . . .

CHAPTER FOURTEEN

A New Transplanting

THE REVEREND FATHER Theodore M. Roessler, brother of Sister Clement Mary, evinced concern over the uncertain state of affairs at Freiburg. His anxiety for the happiness and welfare of his only sister, moved him to contact his old friend and professor of seminary days, when he had studied at the University of Switzerland. And so, at his invitation, the Very Reverend Father Timothy Brauchle, O.F.M. Conv., at that time the Assistant General of the Friars Minor Conventual, in Rome, made inquiry as to the status of the new community at Freiburg.

Father Brauchle found that the community continued to be "on trial" in the Diocese, and that several of its members were in no hurry to secure its formal establishment as a strictly enclosed community belonging to the Second Order of Carmel. His enlightened discernment easily penetrated the miasma of their obscure state and the subsequent dissatisfaction because they were neither this nor that. His keen observation sought out and studied the gentle, refined "little Mother Therese," and noted, too, that she was the recipient of many trials, which indeed, at this point, were hers in abundance. Nor did his experienced eye fail to detect her strong faith in the living God . . . Ah, Mother Therese had long ago mastered the art of casting herself completely upon her Lord, that thus she was able to endure silently and to embrace lovingly, whatever *He* would send her.

"Zelo Zelatus Sum . . ."

Mother Therese was instinctively sincere. Hers was a radiantly winning character, full of candor, open-hearted and straightforward. She had joined the new community with the same ideal in view of leading the strict, hermitical life in the cloister of sacred Carmel.

Carmel to her spelled detachment from all that was not God; it suggested the life of a hermit, in imitation of the holy Prophet Elias, who taught the hermits of Mount Carmel to "live alone with The Alone," and so, give themselves completely to the spirit of silent contemplation. Ah, the future foundress treasured and signally understood Carmel's pure spirit.

"Each one of you is to have a separate cell . . . Each one is to remain in his cell or near it, meditating day and night on the Law of the Lord and watching in prayer." (The Holy Rule) But we must not suppose that Mother Therese's zeal was confined to the solitude of a Carmelite cell. Indeed not! Hers was the zeal that embraced the entire universe. And she was imbued with the idea, nay rather, fully aware of the fact, that one single soul, raised to the state of intimate union with Jesus Crucified, is more useful to the Church, and to the world, than countless others engaged in ceaseless activity.

She loved Carmel's innate silence and its spirit of solitude. Only sincere loyalty therein, she knew, would enable her to keep up an uninterrupted union with her Divine Spouse, Who had taken up His abode in her soul. As time went on, the years only deepened the intensity of her desires. It seems that the Lord alone was her leader and so she was thoroughly permeated by and strengthened with the truth that *He alone* is the inexhaustible Fount of Life, and *He alone* can slake the soul's thirst.

"The Weak Things of the world has
God chosen to put to shame the strong."
(1 Cor. 1: 27.)

Certainly the strange experience of Mother Therese at Freiburg was definitely a painful martyrdom of the heart, nevertheless it was a necessary part of her soul's ever-widening spiritual horizon, and the deepening of its state of transforming union with the Man of Sorrows. She could say with our Mystical Doctor, Saint John of the Cross: "There is no longer anything but the Divine honor and glory." Her patience, too, in dealing with adverse circumstances, was simply heroic. Just when she and her companion, in their peculiar menage, seemed most forlorn and abandoned, Divine Providence signally manifested its wisdom, its power, and its love.

We must admit, however, that up to this time, the so-called "builders" rejected this "hidden jewel," this "valued stone," which would have given, without a doubt, a unique splendour to their "building." But it was the Divine Architect Alone, Who, fashioning His precious masterpiece, took a special delight in keeping the "stone" hidden, unknown, and obscure. He had His plans, and according to His plans, she was destined to become the *corner-stone* in His very House of Prayer. Surely, the "stone" was pleasing to its Maker, and through her faithful correspondence to the Divine Will, there would be an increase of glory to the Triune-God, a harbinger of grace for the souls that would be saved, and a new channel to diffuse the splendour and devotion of the Blessed Virgin Mary of Mount Carmel.

CHAPTER FIFTEEN

Carmel in Naples

THE OLD VINE

FATHER BRAUCHLE's visit to Freiburg brought about a vital turn in the history of our two Carmel-mendicants. His consultation with the Carmelite Superiors in Italy moved the latter to direct Mother Therese and her companion to the Carmel of Saint Bridget in Rome. In reality, they were destined for the Carmel of Naples but to facilitate matters for procuring the necessary permissions from the Holy See, they were to remain for a time in the Roman Carmel. Their stay in this exemplary community, although short-lived, was ever a memorable and edifying experience.

By this time, however, Mother Therese's health had undergone a vast change, and it was easily to be seen that the hot Roman climate was not at all suited to her now greatly-weakened physical condition. Actually, she became so seriously ill, that her life was despaired of. In addition to her increased bodily sufferings, there were other crosses, too. In truth, God tried His trusting child to the very utmost, but His uplifting promise, "My grace is sufficient for thee," like a melody of hope, vibrated unceasingly in the depths of her submissive soul, as the limpid strings of the harmonious lyre respond to the expert touch of the master musician.

She belonged entirely to God, and not for one instant did she ever lose sight of this consoling fact. "Deus solus sufficit," (God Alone suffices) was her symbol of light and of guidance to the very end. Always Divine Providence intervened, and most signally, when black clouds of anxiety and failure seemed to envelop the very destiny of our two "pilgrims."

Among those who venerated the "little Mother Therese" even at this time, was the Carmelite ascetic, the Very Reverend Father Clement Mary of the Guardian Angel, O.C.D., esteemed in the Order for holiness of life, profound learning, and able leadership.

His spiritual direction of our two Carmelites left a special impress upon their souls, and was invaluable. In truth, his kindness and goodness were indescribable, and God sent him to them at a time when they needed him most. Father Clement Mary remained a loyal friend of the foundresses until his saintly death on December 3, 1941.

In the Divine Plan, however, it was the zealous General of the Carmelites, the Most Reverend Father Elias P. Magennis, O. Carm., who was destined to undertake the leadership in the vast enterprise of expanding the vine of the Carmelite nuns of the Ancient Observance to the West. In his zeal for the glory of his Order, and out of love for the Queen of Carmel, Father Magennis had long envisioned the idea of founding a Calced Carmel for cloistered nuns in America. He knew for a certainty that America's young womanhood, those inspired by the Almighty, would be drawn irresistibly to the Marian cloisters, where they would dedicate their youth, and their entire lives, to the holy service of Mary's Son, Our Lord and Saviour, JESUS CHRIST, by fervent prayer, penance, and hidden sacrifice. And so, his choice for the responsibility of such an undertaking, fell upon the little Mother Therese of Jesus, and her companion, Sister Clement Mary of the Guardian Angel.

Father Magennis, assigned to special work at the Vatican, likewise enjoyed the personal friendship of the beloved Pontiff, Pius XI. It was Father Magennis who was largely instrumental in hastening the permissions from the Holy See, to transfer our two "pilgrims" to the Carmel in Naples, to the ancient Monastery of "Santa Croce di Lucca," located in the charming Coast-city, overlooking the colorful Bay of Naples. Here, in the healthy, vibrant, Neapolitan air, Mother Therese's health was sufficiently restored to enable her, with her young companion, to share in the full-blooming ascetic life of this venerable community. However she was never to regain her former state of good health but like her valiant Patroness, Saint Teresa of Avila, she did not allow her weakened constitution, nor the constant ill-health to deter her in her apostolic life and great labors for Christ.

And so, in the revered Carmel of Naples, in the sacred cloister of the old monastery named in honor of the "Holy Cross of Lucca," Mother Therese of Jesus and Sister Clement Mary were prepared to be the instruments of God, to bring a new Garden of MARY to the soil of America.

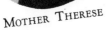

MOTHER THERESE   MOTHER CLEMENT MARY

The Foundresses of the Carmel at Allentown

Facade and Main Entrance of the Little Flower
Shrine-Chapel of Allentown

PART III

Carmel of Allentown

"But it was the Divine Architect Alone, Who, fashioning
His precious masterpiece, took a special delight in keeping the
'stone' hidden, unknown, and obscure. He had His plans, and
according to His plans, she was destined to become the *corner-
stone* in His very House of Prayer . . ."

"She has left behind her a monument in the erection of your Monastery, but still more, in the religious formation, which she gave to her Community."

Dennis Cardinal Dougherty,
Archbishop of Philadelphia.

CHAPTER SIXTEEN

First American Foundation

STRANGE AS it may seem, Divine Providence used the earthquake of July 23, 1930, to hasten further the inception of the great enterprise. The fearful eruptions of Mount Vesuvius wrought great havoc in the surrounding towns and ports. The old Monastery of the Carmelites, dating back to 1536, as we have noted, had to be vacated during the volcanic disturbances, which threatened to demolish the ancient edifice of Carmel.

Meanwhile, the nuns were compelled to seek safety and shelter in a small villa near the sea. In these cramped quarters, that would scarcely accommodate a family of six, the thirty "refugees" from Carmel huddled together. Indeed, they were provided with splendid opportunities for the practice of self-renunciation and limitless sacrifice. Mother Therese and her companion likewise manifested true heroism during these trying times. In truth, their edifying examples proved that penance was simply second nature to them, so well did they make the best of every inconvenience and painful circumstance, for love of Him Who is pleased to give . . . and to take away!

It was at this very point that the distinguished Carmelite General, the Most Reverend Father Elias Magennis, O. Carm., completed the necessary arrangements for the founding of the first Monastery of the cloistered Carmelite Nuns of the Ancient Observance, in the United States. Father Magennis would brook no further delay, and urged Mother Therese and her companion to start out immediately on the long ocean voyage that would bring them to Western shores.

Father Elias Magennis, O. Carm.

We cannot help, in the course of our narrative, referring frequently, and with filial affection, to this outstanding Carmelite, Father Magennis, who succeeded so admirably in imparting to others the spirit of zeal that burned so strongly in his heart.

It was this same Father Magennis, O. Carm., who was ever the most faithful friend and competent advisor of the two grateful foundresses, as he was the life-long friend and much-valued counsellor of the well-known Mother Mary Joseph Butler, of Marymount. In fact, it was under his authoritative help that Mother Butler purchased and established her first Roman House, on Via Nomentana, which, Father Magennis declared, "would become the most beautiful House in your Institute."

Nor can we do otherwise than relate here the remarkable words of the Supreme Pontiff, of happy memory,

Benedict XV, spoken of the illustrious Carmelite, Father Magennis, on the occasion of his election to the General-ship of the Carmelite Order:

> "The winter for CARMEL is now over: as under the beneficent rays of the spring-sun, nature bursts forth into verdant bloom, so the administration of Father Magennis will usher in, we pray, the spring-time of growth and new life, for the ORDER of CARMEL."

Prophetic words, indeed, of a saintly Pontiff, which words have come true!

BON VOYAGE

It was on October 15, 1930, the feast of the seraphic virgin of Carmel, Saint Teresa of Avila, that permission was granted by the Sacred Congregation of Religious, whereby the Reverend Mother Therese of Jesus and Sister Clement Mary of the Guardian Angel were canonically commissioned to found a Calced Carmelite Monastery of Papal Enclosure in America. And the two apparently insignificant nuns, relying entirely on the mercy of Divine Providence, did not hesitate to commence their enormous task. Unafraid of the cross-laden future, with twelve heavy trunks that contained "everything but a monastery building," they embarked in Naples, on the steamer "Providence," to sail for the fair land of America.

The worthy General, Father Magennis, had planned to accompany them to the steamer, but his special assignments at the Vatican, at that particular time, compelled him to forego this great pleasure. He appointed two representatives, in the persons of his able Assistant (later his successor in the Generalship), the Very Reverend Hilary Maria Doswald, O. Carm., of Rome, and the Very Reverend Andrew Ciampa, O. Carm., Prior of Carmine Maggiore, in Naples, to conduct the foundresses to the steamer.

Some Interesting Stops

Gliding over the placid blue waters of the Mediterranean, the steamer made a few stops, which enabled the two courageous "pilgrims" to visit, first of all, the picturesque coast-city of Palermo. Here the nuns spent a few hours on land, visiting the well-known Monastery of the Calced Carmelites, and they also made an excursion to beautiful Monreale, situated on the mountaintop. From this high elevation, the nuns beheld the awful grandeur of mountain and valley scenery, and an outstanding view of the serene bay below.

The vast spectacle of the broad expanse of waters, mirroring the light of the glowing sun, and the azure of the Italian sky, seemed to send scintillating rays heavenward, like a trail of light ascending to the heavens. As their gaze lingered on this scenic splendour, our two "pilgrims" marvelled at the nonpareil beauty and incomparable wonder of God's creations, and their thoughts turned to heaven and to the Divine Artist, Who sends forth His shafts of love and grace, illuminating the hearts of His children, on earth below.

ALGIERS IN AFRICA

The next stop was at Algiers, in French Africa, on November 2. Here the two nuns assisted at Holy Mass, in the great Cathedral of Saint Philip, and heard a fervent sermon in French.

LISBON IN PORTUGAL

A third stop was made at Lisbon, in Portugal. Before going ashore, our travellers were informed, to their utter amazement, that religious garb was forbidden for public wear. The intrepid Mother Therese, and her likewise fearless companion, were not at all dismayed, but with redoubled courage, set out, in their Carmelite attire, for a tour of the city.

The sight of the two nuns, in their long, black veils, and religious habits, caused quite a sensation. Within a few minutes, they were followed by an admirable "escort" of Portuguese men, women and children, who, it seemed, welcomed this grand opportunity to display their filial allegiance to their deep-rooted and invincible Faith.

Old Monastery of Saint Jerome

Seeing themselves protected by this impenetrable, though human, "wall," our two daring "pilgrims" waxed strong in courage, and decided to penetrate even to the suburbs of Lisbon, in order to visit the once-hallowed Monastery of Saint Jerome, in a place called Belem.

This old Monastery dates back to the year 1500, and was built to immortalize the discovery, by Vasco da Gama, of a sea-route, to India, 1497-1499. The ancient building is of white stone, and the style of architecture is a mixture of Gothic, Renaissance and Moorish, truly outstandingly beautiful in its superb symmetry, and harmonious grandeur. The façade in particular is artistically decorated.

It may be noted here, and to our profound sorrow, that all the important buildings of Lisbon are, or have been, churches or monasteries, but owing to governmental suppression, May 28, 1834, these precious structures and sacred monasteries have been used mainly as barracks. So the extensive tour of Lisbon was a profoundly sad disappointment to our two faithful daughters of Mother Church, who had to witness the degradation of these once-singularly-sacred buildings, that were snatched by unkind hands, and put to profane use.

Chapter Seventeen

On American Soil

On November 13, the sturdy "Providence" reached Providence, Rhode Island, the first landing-point, of our two "pilgrims"—in the New World. However, it was on the Feast of ALL SAINTS of the CARMEL-ITE ORDER, November 14, 1930, that the actual place of disembarkation was reached at the New York pier.

Sheltered At Englewood

Here they were met, and warmly welcomed by the Carmelite Fathers, who represented the North American and the New York Provinces. The three who took the lead in welcoming the newcomers were: the Very Reverend Lawrence D. Flanagan, O. Carm., Provincial of the Saint Elias Province, New York City; the Very Reverend Silverius J. Quigley, O. Carm., Assistant Provincial of the Province of the Most Pure Heart of Mary, Englewood, New Jersey; and the Reverend Michael J. Christie, O. Carm., also of New York.

One of the Fathers, when asked to arrange for the shipment of the twelve heavy trunks belonging to the foundresses, could not conceal his utter amazement, and he replied: "Two little nuns, and twelve heavy trunks!" And he gave them a broad smile.

At last they were on American soil! And their hearts were filled with gratitude, when, after being escorted to Englewood by the Carmelite Fathers, they were offered sisterly hospitality by the Reverend Mother Mary Agatha of the Sisters of Saint Joseph of Newark, at Englewood Cliffs, New Jersey.

These excellent and fervent religious were the first to open their convent and their hearts' generosity to the two daughters of Carmel. And it is well to mention here that the twelve heavy trunks followed the "pilgrims," slowly but surely, to their proper destination, through the noble kindness of a Jewish friend of the Carmelites. The Sisters of Saint Joseph remained devoted and generous benefactors of Carmel, presenting the Sisters with their first Ostensorium, candlesticks, and other beautiful furnishings for their future sanctuary.

The Sisters at Graymoor

Mother Therese and Sister Clement Mary had a grand reception at Graymoor, New York, where they spent some time with the Sisters of the Atonement. The exemplary Foundress, Reverend Mother Lurana Mary Frances, received the Carmelites most cordially, and it was through her maternal kindness that the first altar with tabernacle was given to the new Carmel, together with a complete set of Church vestments.

Dominicans at Paterson

The Dominican Sisters, on Jackson Street, also rendered wonderful assistance. Reverend Mother M. Ida, O.P., superior of the Convent, was most kind, and supplied material for habits and clothing.

Mother Therese and Sister Clement Mary peered into the future, as it were, and pictured to themselves the new Carmelite community, at work in the monastery gardens. Hence, they would welcome old habits, used clothing, and the like. It was always Mother Ida who came "to the rescue," supplying habits of *white wool,* which could be, and were, easily transformed to a humble Carmelite *brown.* The Carmelites were glad and grateful to make use of everything.

The Right Reverend Monsignor Adalbert Frey, V.F., spiritual Director of the Dominicans at Paterson, often came forward with a generous benefaction, and proved himself a lasting friend.

Good Shepherd Nuns at Peekskill

At the Convent of the Good Shepherd Nuns, in Peekskill, New York, the fervent Prioress, Reverend Mother Mary Dolorosa, gave them a most affectionate and cordial welcome. Her maternal solicitude for the

Sisters of the Blessed Virgin Mary of Mount Carmel prompted her to present the nuns with the first statue of the Virgin, Our Lady, to grace an altar in the future Carmel.

Moreover, it was Mother Dolorosa's far-seeing kindness that inspired her to furnish the necessary dishes, china-ware, and other needed items for both kitchen and pantry. Her keen eye missed none of these details.

FELICIAN SISTERS AT LODI

Gracious and bountiful hospitality was afforded the Carmelites by the Mother Provincial and her Sisters, at the Convent of the Felician Sisters, Lodi, New Jersey. Reverend Mother Mary Angelica and her dear community, could not do enough to assist the work of the Carmelite foundation. Through her unlimited kindness, the first supplies of clothing materials for Carmel's future candidates were generously provided, together with many other practical items, too numerous to mention here.

"OUTSIDE MISSION WORK"

Certainly our two Carmelites were most deeply grateful for the countless favors and numberless benefactions received from the many friends of Carmel, and it would be impossible to name each individual, each convent, each Community, who so gladly responded to their needs. But to those who know something of the meditative life of Carmel, it will be easily understood when we say that the intrepid Mother Therese and Sister Clement Mary must have felt worse than weary and foot-sore.

However, the indefatigable spirit of the Foundress was never worn out. Nevertheless, to endure the constant journeys, the endless goings and comings, the diverse foods, and the like, certainly provided them with many an opportunity for self-renunciation.

They welcomed the evening hours, when they would seek the solitude of their rooms, to taste again the quiet peace and cloister-like stillness; to indulge to the full in holy meditation and fervent prayer. True, this "outside mission work" had to be accomplished. It was a part, and a necessary part, of their great enterprise. But we cannot refrain from mentioning that our courageous "pilgrims" longed for the day when they would be in their own cherished convent, away from the turmoil of outside affairs, safe, and secluded in their Garden-Enclosed, in their Carmel-solitude, and life of unceasing prayer.

And it must not be imagined that this manner of procuring material aid and friends for the new foundation, was not without its thorns, and, sometimes, very sharp ones, too! But, even the thorns would have their special place in the great enterprise, and formed an important link in the establishment of a work that would, undoubtedly, bring great glory to the good God.

Gift From the Little King

The fervent Discalced Sisters of Carmel had long been in operation in the Philadelphia Archdiocese. However, His Eminence, Dennis Cardinal Dougherty, known for his outstanding missionary zeal, and for his singular devotion to the "Little Flower" of Carmel, could not fail to welcome a foundation of the Carmelites of the Ancient Observance into his Archdiocese. And this welcome was made all the more certain, since the Calced Carmelites intended to dedicate their new Monastery to this glorious daughter of Carmel, SAINT THERESE OF THE CHILD JESUS

On December 17, 1930, Mother Therese of Jesus, and Sister Clement Mary, were granted an audience with His Eminence, Dennis Cardinal Dougherty, the truly zealous and gracious Archbishop of Philadelphia.

Little Therese, who faithfully looked after her two devoted proteges, was not slow in revealing her consoling proximity on this very memorable occasion, and really, her "roses," upon her two valiant sisters in Carmel she let fall in torrents. Wonderful, indeed, and most significant, too, that on the eve of the Birthday of the Little King, December 24, 1930, the required document was signed by His Eminence, Cardinal Dougherty, permitting Mother Therese and Sister Clement Mary to establish, in the Archdiocese of Philadelphia, a Carmel of the Ancient Observance.

Mother Angelica of the Felician Order had a convent of her Sisters at Reading, Pennsylvania. She, therefore, directed Mother Therese and her companion to Reading, in well-known Berks County.

Father Hammeke

At Reading, the two nuns made the acquaintance of the venerable Pastor of Saint Paul's Church, the Reverend Father William Hammeke, whose limitless acts of kindness would fill many pages of this humble history.

From his first meeting with the Carmelites, Father Hammeke remained their loyal and staunch friend and great benefactor. And with respect and grateful devotion, we wish to remark here, that Father Hammeke was a faithful friend all through the years, even when, at 85 years of age, weighed down with years and illness, resulting from a severe stroke which brought him to the brink of the grave, he still managed to smile and to be witty. He recovered his health at that time, sufficiently, to be allowed to make a trip to Allentown, to visit the Carmelites on June 28, 1947. And he greeted Mother Clement Mary with the cheery words: "Oh, come back to Reading!"

Really, his exquisite kindness knew no bounds, and he became so enthusiastic and interested in a Carmelite foundation, that he spared neither time nor efforts to help the Sisters choose a site, in or about Reading.

In fact, it was Father Hammeke's solicitude that provided them with a first little "convent," if we may call it such. And that was in an orphanage! But he considered them as "orphans"—they had no home of their own, and so he felt inspired to offer them the vacant orphanage near Saint Paul's. And since the good Sisters of Christian Charity were located near-by, and thrilled at the nearness of the Carmelites, it was suggested that Mother Therese and Sister Clement Mary take up temporary quarters in the orphanage. And this they really did!

It would take pages to record the many instances of kindness, warm-heartedness and sincere reception afforded the Carmelites by the Reading people, guided and inspired as they were by their zealous Pastor, the Reverend Father Hammeke, and by the fervent, generous Sisters of Christian Charity.

Chapter Eighteen

"O Felix Allentown"

IN THE MEANTIME, the Cardinal Archbishop commis-sioned the Right Reverend Monsignor Leo Gregory Fink, V.F., Rector of the Sacred Heart Church, Allen-town, to assist the nuns in the selection of a suitable site for the new Monastery. Eventually, both His Eminence and Monsignor Fink named *LANARK MANOR*, a charming, picturesque suburb of Allentown, as the choice site and ideal location for a Monastery, dedicated to the contemplative life of Carmel. Thus directed by Monsignor Fink, Mother Therese purchased the Weibel Estate, at Lanark Manor, which comprised about five acres of land, a spacious residence containing seventeen rooms, a large four-car stone garage, and an artesian well to provide an excellent water-supply.

SOME DIFFICULTIES

Superbly ideal as the site was, the project of locating in this particular vicinity engendered many heartaches. Not to mention the severance of friendly, sincere ties in Reading, the idea of the "water supply" created a seem-ingly insurmountable obstacle. The artesian well on the new premises was supplying water to the whole valley, numbering about sixteen or more houses, scattered throughout the area. And this task of supplying water to the surrounding area was no small obligation for the cloistered nuns.

Through the gracious ingenuity of Attorney James C. Lanshe, representing the Monastery, and the refined kindliness of attitude of Attorney Karl Y. Donecker, representing the Lanark Water Association, an amicable agreement was drawn up, protecting the Monastery and its water-rights. However, this was not an overnight-task, but, actually, a problem that took several years to untangle, until finally the difficulties were ironed out satisfactorily.

And there were other drawbacks, too, especially the lack of sympathy of many of the neighbors, and even their open hostility. Some were not at all in harmony with the idea of having *cloistered nuns* dwelling in their midst.

Even Mr. Weibel, the owner of the Lanark Estates, was most reluctant to sell his property to "religious women," and he showed a bitter countenance to Mother Therese and to her companion when they were inspecting the property. But, then, he had never spoken to a Religious in his whole life. His ideas were very strange in regard to nuns. In spite of himself, he was deeply impressed by the charming personality of Mother Ther-

118

ese, and by the unassuming sweetness of her gentle companion.

Later on, when called to the Monastery on business matters, he made this admission: "I never realized that *nuns* could be so lovely." He showed a respectful esteem for the two foundresses, despite his original ideas.

"Saint Therese's Valley"

On May 22, 1931, the two Carmelites motored to Allentown. But what a sad departure! Father Hammeke, who had long contemplated the unspeakable good that would result from a Carmelite "power-house" of prayer in the vicinity of Reading, actually sobbed to see them depart. Nevertheless, even at this crucial point, Mother Therese's humour was at hand, and she remarked to her dear companion, that it was quite fitting that an undertaker, from Allentown, should have the pleasure of bringing the Sisters to their new home.

There was nothing remarkable about the trip, but the heat on that day was so intense that halfway to Allentown, the car would not move anymore. After the necessary cooling, and re-oiling, the car resumed its course. Arrived at Allentown, the Sisters called on Monsignor Fink, the Vicar Forane, at the Sacred Heart Rectory. Monsignor appointed the Reverend John P. N. Fries, Rector of Saint Joseph's Church, Limeport, to conduct the nuns to Lanark Manor.

LANARK MANOR is situated about four and one-half miles from the city of ALLENTOWN, and lies, snugly and tranquilly, at the foot of the Blue Ridge Mountains, which encircle part of the valley, like a friendly enclosure wall.

It was MARY'S Month of MAY. Plants of various kind, flowers of indescribable beauty, trees, graceful and stately, shrubbery, varied and unique, presented an almost ethereal sight. Even the terrific heat was tempered to moderation in this serene spot. A refreshing breeze seemed to play about the trees, causing them, especially the tall poplars, to sway gently, and to throw tantalizing shadows, here and there. Sweet-smelling flowers, too, nodded their heads in undisturbed contentment.

Undoubtedly, LANARK MANOR, at first sight, presented an enchanting picture, and Mother Therese said: "It is SAINT THERESE'S VALLEY!" And the nuns were immediately impressed with the majestic silence that prevailed in the scenic valley, a silence broken only by the joyous notes of little birds, welcoming the "pioneers," and warbling their sweet melody to the skies, as a grateful homage to their Adorable Creator. Their perpetual song intensified the sacred stillness, and enhanced the charm of the utter peacefulness and placid serenity that greeted our zealous Carmelites upon their advent into the sylvan valley.

120

"At all times I will bless the Lord; His praise shall be on my lips continually." (Ps. 33, 2.)

The large, quiet Manor had a stately appearance, and presented an admirable picture to the nuns, as they approached the driveway. There was no one to greet them, besides the birds, and flowers, and trees, as mentioned heretofore. No one was there to welcome them!

Mother Therese and Sister Clement Mary entered the Manor together. The house was absolutely empty, possessing nothing but its bare walls, vacant rooms, still corridors, and its profound silence! The foundresses enjoyed its utter emptiness, reminding them, as it did, of the Little King's Bethlehem, where even the necessaries were lacking. This was holy Poverty indeed! But Poverty was always a source of real delight to them who knew how to drink deeply at the fount of privation, and to taste the ineffable joy which always accompanies trials and crosses generously accepted. Indeed, the foundresses took care that *Poverty* should be the touchstone of their glorious undertaking.

They toured the whole house. Ah, here was something! The keen eye of Mother Therese sighted a can of ashes in the basement. With a merry twinkle in her eyes and in her voice, she exclaimed to her wondering companion: "Now, Sister, we can do penance in sackcloth and ashes!"

LANARK MANOR ESTATE

"First" Convent of the Carmelites in
Saint Therese's Valley

CHAPTER NINETEEN

Planning the Monastery

EVERY NOOK and corner of the house was carefully examined, and all the while, Mother Therese was making plans. The large entrance room would serve admirably for a temporary chapel for the public. And the adjoining sun-parlor, bright and cheery, would make an excellent nuns' choir (cloistered chapel). These two compartments were already separated by a door which needed only a small iron grating to be inserted, since it is through the iron grille that the cloistered nun receives her Eucharistic Lord. Of course, these temporary accommodations would be very cramped, but they would do for the present.

At the extreme left of the entrance, alongside the hallway, was a large room, and Mother Therese intended this for a sacristy, and, when occasion demanded, for a dining-room for the convenience of visitors. Also, at the left of the entrance, was a wide, open stairway. Here, on the first landing, they would place the exquisitely beautiful Shrine-group of the Little Flower. And the wide, mounting steps would serve as tiers to hold the flower-vases, the candelabra, and the votive lights that would flicker before the Shrine.

Another large room, next to the sacristy, could be converted into a convent-parlor, where business affairs would be transacted, and where visitors could come to interview the nuns, to find solace in their trials, and to imbibe encouragement and new spiritual vigor.

And the parlor, too, would have to be partitioned off to provide another wing to serve as a tiny speak-room, from which part of the enclosed monastery the cloistered nun would handle business matters, or converse, when necessary, with visitors and with those seeking spiritual counsel. This small room would require, also, a window with an iron grating, to be covered with a thick black curtain over the inside grate of wood, so that there would be no view from within or from without. Here, also, would have to be installed a "turn" (revolving shelf, so to speak), through which letters, or other articles, could be handed in or out of the monastery.

The next room was large enough to serve for a pantry, and this led to the large and pleasant kitchen, on the right side of which was another room, that could be utilized as a "cell" for one of the nuns. Really, the plans of the Foundress could not have been improved upon, but were carried out to the smallest detail. Suffice it to say, that the second and third floors were destined for dormitories, for the future candidates of Carmel.

For the present, the cooking could be done in the basement, where there was a large, airy room, at the foot of the stairway. But, as yet, there was no stove in the house. In fact, there was not even a chair on which to sit, there was no table, there was not the smallest dish to be found! And there was no bed in the house! But these utter privations did not in the least disturb the "pioneers." They were very tired, of course, after touring and examining the big house, and before that, the long, hot, weary journey from Reading, in a car that, in the fierce heat, had resembled a baking-oven. And they had not tasted any food or water since early that morning. This was self-forgetfulness in practice! But, really, we may epitomize the entire spiritual life of this valiant Daughter of Carmel, in the short, but deeply significant phrase: "she forgot self."

REFECTORY VS. LAUNDRY

It was quite convenient for the two nuns to take their meagre refections in the little laundry room, at the back of the house. In a very short time, however, these quarters proved extremely cramped, so that it was found necessary to enlarge the laundry room in order to make it serve also as a decent refectory (dining-room).

On wash days, the simple furniture of tables and chairs was moved into the extreme corner of the room, so as to make space for the laundry tubs, the buckets, and other laundry utensils.

KITCHEN IN THE GARAGE

Still later, when Mother Therese singled out the large stone garage for the permanent novitiate wing, it was found imperative to transfer the community kitchen to the northwest part of the big garage. Ever solicitous for the comfort and health of the nuns, the superiors were always scrupulously careful that all the planning and arrangement should further and benefit their spiritual and physical welfare.

Since the garage was situated about two hundred feet away from the Manor, the youthful nuns of Carmel were always enthusiastic about the endless "processions," from the garage to the refectory, to transport the food, to and fro, in a little wagon, or by hand, as the case required. (Six young candidates were, by this time, members of the young Community.) At times, however, it really was a great inconvenience, but it did provide plenty of healthful exercise for the young Carmelites. It would require many pages were we to relate the countless instances of inevitable merriment, and even disaster, that took place on these endless "processions."

One, in particular, was the "journey" of a young Sister, carrying in her arms a large roaster-pan, filled with steaming, hot macaroni for the conventual dinner. It was winter. The snow-covered road concealed a strip of ice. And so, before the unsuspecting Sister realized her

126

step, she slipped on the icy road, and went down into the snow. She had presence of mind to try to hold on to the macaroni. But, alas, her efforts were futile. As she went down, the pan of macaroni flew into the air, and its tasty contents scattered all about the ground. Then, to top it off, and before the poor Sister could gather herself together, out rushed the hungry goose, the gander, with their little "army" of goslings, and they consumed the macaroni. Mother Therese, ever ready to encourage and to console, smoothed out the incident in her usual kindness, saying: "It is all right, Sister. We will open some cans!"

And Still Later

It will be interesting to add here that the east wing of the garage was used as a protecting-shelter for a number of chickens, the gift of kind friends. The chicks were thus privileged to share the seclusion of the cloister, and a close proximity to the happy nuns. However, when it was found possible to do so, the chickens were moved to a more practical "residence," on the right side of the big garden, almost at the end of the wide-open plot. A little later, a shed was attached to the first chicken compartment to house three little goats, that would provide the nuns with milk.

The thick cement walls separating the different compartments of the garage did not permit any penetrating odors. Thus the middle compartment was reserved for a "work-room" for the nuns, and when necessity arose, also as a laundry room. The loft, over the garage, served as a storage place, where corn and other things were stored for drying. The dry husks were intended for the mattresses used by the Carmelites for their meagre repose on a little bed of three boards resting on two "horses." Though not the ladder of perfection, there was a scaling ladder in the garage, which the young nuns had to use in climbing up and down, in order to reach the loft.

AN ADDITION

Meanwhile, Mother Therese found it necessary to construct a closed-in hall-way, at the east side of the house, to serve as a temporary cloister-walk, permitting the enclosed nuns to go from the refectory room to the choir, since it had to be a private entrance, reserved, of course, for the use of the cloistered sisters. Only a few days had elapsed, when a kind friend came forth and presented a gas-range to the nuns, for their monastery kitchen. "God will provide" evinces a healthy optimism, and this trusting expression was like a melody in the heart of Mother Therese, and was ever on her lips. Her fervent companion re-echoed the song, and so, their spirit of "dependence on God's Providence," grew with their growth.

Also, on the same evening of their arrival, as the two "stalwart hermits" looked forward to a hard bed on the floor, they received a most unexpected surprise. Two little cots were sent them from the Sacred Heart Hospital, at Allentown. Monsignor Fink, carefully noting the large as well as the small details of this splendid enterprise, and inspired by Heaven, no doubt, felt certain of their practicability. And, indeed, they were most welcome!

God's shielding love and His most tender Providence *always* provided for His two grateful "proteges" . . . The Lord Jesus was only keeping His sweet word to those who had "left all things" to follow Him, in His apostolic life of prayer, and sacrifice . . . for souls. And so, His Hundredfold of grace, of peace, and of blessing, was theirs in abundance.

Certainly the first scenes of this noble foundation of Carmel at Allentown remind us forcibly of those which have been immortalized by the facile pen of another heroic foundress, the great Saint Teresa of Avila, whose consuming and untiring zeal burned vividly in the hearts and souls of her successors in Carmel. And they, like her, would try to build their spiritual edifice upon sacrifice, suffering, and prayer. They hoped their sowing would bring forth good fruit! True enough, the Manor was not intended for a Carmelite cloister, but, as has been noted, it did serve as an excellent place to start.

*Mother Therese of Jesus and Sister Clement Mary
at the Formal Opening of the New Carmel*

*Procession at Formal Opening of Allentown Carmel
on June 18, 1931*

CHAPTER TWENTY

First Mass and Solemn Opening

AFTER THEIR arrival at Lanark Manor, on the first three mornings, the two nuns heard Mass and received Holy Communion at Saint Joseph's Church, in Limeport. On the fourth day, May 26, which happened to be the transferred Feast of Saint Mary Magdalen di Pazzi, the First Holy Mass was celebrated in the new Carmel of Allentown by the Prior General of the Carmelite Order, the Most Reverend Father Elias P. Magennis, O. Carm., from Rome. Father Magennis likewise presided at the Solemn Benediction of the Most Blessed Sacrament, assisted by the Reverend Silverius J. Quigley, O. Carm., and the Reverend Michael J. Christie, O. Carm.

HERE DWELLS ETERNAL LOVE

And the King of Kings, Our Lord JESUS CHRIST, from that day on, was enthroned in the Tabernacle, and took up His abode in this new Sanctuary of Love, in sacred Carmel. What a source of delight, what an uplift of zest and fortitude His Divine Presence brought to His two spouses, who shared the ineffable joy of preparing

131

the lovely and artistic silk trimmings for the Tabernacle. They deemed it a labor of love for the Saviour, and a real privilege to adorn His new Eucharistic Throne.

Pope Pius Blesses

Mother Therese and Sister Clement Mary were hardly three days at Lanark Manor, when they received a cablegram, coming directly from His Holiness, POPE PIUS XI, who had received the two foundresses in a special audience before they had left Italy.

It read as follows:

Citta del Vaticano
May 25, 1931

"CARMELITE SISTERS — Occasion Opening Your First House in America, Holy Father cordially grants whole Community Apostolic Blessing."

Cardinal Pacelli.

The above was followed by a cable from His Eminence, Cardinal Cerretti, also of the Vatican:

"My Blessing and My Best Wishes—"

Cardinal Cerretti.

Another cable arrived, from the Roman Curia of the Carmelite Order, and signed by the Assistant General, the Very Reverend Hilary Maria Doswald, O. Carm.:

"Congratulations and Prayers—"

Curia Doswald.

FORMAL OPENING

Monsignor Fink, who had been appointed the Diocesan Visitor of the Carmelites, arranged for the formal opening of the new House, and for an impressive outdoor celebration. The affair was scheduled for June 18th. It was a singularly beautiful event. Solemn Benediction of the Most Blessed Sacrament was celebrated by Monsignor Fink, on an improvised altar, flanked by stately trees and graceful flowers, on the spacious grounds. The Reverend Charles F. Keller, J.C.D., and Reverend Edward Reichl, M.S.C., assisted the Monsignor. The Very Reverend Patrick Russell, O. Carm., of New York City, delivered the sermon.

Over two thousand people were present. Special cars conveyed the people from Allentown, Bethlehem, and vicinity, through special arrangements made by Monsignor Fink. Reading and Philadelphia friends, likewise, came in great numbers. Special buses brought friends and visitors from New York and New Jersey.

In the procession were a great number of the Clergy, also, a dozen or so altar boys, and little girls in white, the children of Mary from Sacred Heart parish, Allentown. Then came our two Religious of Carmel, with downcast eyes, holding in one hand, a blessed candle, and the other was shielded beneath the Brown Scapular. There were a countless number of Sisters, representing

133

the different Congregations in the vicinity, and then, the laity. All carried candles. And it reminded onlookers of the unique processions in the hallowed Grotto of Lourdes in France.

One who was present on this memorable occasion, mentioned that all eyes were turned on the two humble Carmelites, in their coarse brown robes, pure white mantles, and long black veils, looking devout and calm, with their pale, ascetic faces and recollected mien. Their very appearance, everything about them, inspired reverence and noble elevation of thought. Their peaceful, lowered gaze showed no interest in the glamour of the occasion. They shunned the publicity of it all. And they would have been unspeakably glad to hide in some forgotten corner in their silent cloister rather than to face this glare of the outer world. However, the lamp of Faith burned brightly in their hearts. And Mother Therese's answer calmed the disquietude of her gentle companion: "Sister, this too is the Will of God!"

Two Candidates

Who would have dreamed that in this immense throng of people, Our Lord was making His way among the crowd, and secretly, known only to Himself, was selecting two little girls, aged about fourteen and fifteen respectively, to be future candidates for this sacred Carmel, and to be among the first spiritual daughters of

Mother Therese! Was it not fitting that Christ should choose His spouses, first of all, from the little town which He so honored, by placing on its border, a Monastery of CARMEL?

IMMEDIATE GROWTH

Shortly after the official opening of the Carmel, a number of candidates presented themselves, so that, before long, the little community numbered about eleven Sisters. Also, four nuns from the Monastery of Santa Croce di Lucca, Naples, were sent to the Allentown Carmel to help out, and after two years, they returned to their Convent in Italy.

To seclude the nuns from the outside world, the entire property was closed in by a nine-foot fence. This protecting wall afforded the much-needed privacy after the expansion work was begun. It met with disapproval among the neighbors, who openly criticized the high wall, and someone went so far as to insert an article in a small advertisement paper in Allentown, questioning the necessity of a high wall to enclose the nuns.

MANUAL WORK

A large section of the land was reserved for a garden patch. It was tilled at once, and the results showed that Mother Therese and Sister Clement Mary were good farmers. They raised vegetables of all kinds to carry

135

them over the long winter months. But this was simply following securely their Holy Rule, which prescribes that: "You should always do some work that the devil may always find you occupied and not be able to gain any entrance into your hearts on account of your idleness. You have in this both the teaching and example of Saint Paul, the Apostle, by whose mouth Christ has spoken and who was appointed and given by God as 'Preacher and Doctor of the Gentiles in Faith and in truth.' If you follow him, you cannot go astray. 'In labor and in toil,' he says, 'we were among you, working day and night lest we should be chargeable to any of you. Not as if we had not the power, but that we might give ourselves a pattern unto you to imitate us.'" (Chapter XV)

Hard work or easy work, the Superiors rolled up their sleeves, and the young candidates were quick to follow their good example, so that all shared in the work of the Monastery.

THE NOVITIATE

Mother Therese's plan to have the large stone garage converted into the first wing of the real Monastery, was put into effect on April 19, 1934, when the work of construction was begun. On August 19, this building was solemnly blessed by the Right Reverend Monsignor Leo G. Fink, V.F., of Allentown. He was assisted by the Very Reverend Chrysostom J. Anderson, O. Carm., of Chicago, and by the Reverend John F. Wiesler, of Allentown. Then, on September 8, the Feast of Our Lady's Nativity, the first novices were installed in the novitiate wing of the Monastery.

THE INTERIOR

On the main floor of the Novitiate, we find a large refectory, the kitchen, and a small pantry. The second floor contains fourteen cells, destined for the novices and postulants. These cells flank the long corridor, at one end of which is the little "hermitage" of Our Lady of Peace. Seven additional cells and a large recreation room make up the third floor.

CARMELITE CELL

The cell is very simple. The furniture consists of a bed, made of two trestles supporting a platform of three boards on which is placed a mattress of corn husks and a straw pillow. A crucifix of wood, a small picture of Our Lady of Mount Carmel, and another of Saint Therese of the Child Jesus, are the only ornaments. The cell also contains a small table, a wooden chair, a holy water font, and a copy of the Rule and Constitutions.

THE MAUSOLEUM

Urged by inspiration, Mother Therese wished to provide a suitable burying place for the new Carmel. A little group of nuns undertook the task of building a beautiful crypt of stone. Mr. Theodore Reybitz, a teacher in the Bethlehem High School, together with his several friends, finished the building. As it stands now, the mausoleum looks, from a distance, like a tiny chapel, having little stained glass windows (the gift of Rev. Father Hammeke), and a neat altar in it, in the center of which is enthroned a large Crucifix. Little did the holy Foundress suspect that she would be the first to be interred there.

Had she not directly provided for the vault, the very first Sister to die would have been buried in an outside cemetery, and that would have meant a separation from the very beginning. The foreseeing Mother wished to avoid this. Thus, the timely erection of the crypt found provision ready for the emergency.

"Necessity Has No Law"

The Incomparable Mother of Carmel, MARY IM-MACULATE, inflamed many young hearts to respond to the call to the interior life of Her Order, so that it was imperative for Mother Therese to provide immediately for a complete Monastery. Her happy group of nuns, aided by generous volunteers, became diggers, carpenters, plasterers, painters, electricians, and general laborers for the growing Carmel. One Sister even became official "boiler-man."

It must be admitted that sacrifice was not a matter of surprise to these generous souls who, inspired and encouraged by the stimulating example of the exemplary foundresses, welcomed the occasions of self-sacrifice, the countless privations, and untold inconveniences. They worked and prayed together with true fervor of spirit, and despite the enormous activity, Mother Therese and Sister Clement Mary saw to it that they followed the strict observance of the Rule, and kept intact their enclosure as far as was possible in their unconventional surroundings.

THE REFECTORY

Refectory, or Nuns' Dining Hall, Carmel of the Little Flower,
Allentown, Pa.

CARMELITE CELL

Cell of a Cloistered Nun, Carmelite Monastery,
Saint Therese's Valley, Allentown, Pa.

CHAPTER TWENTY-ONE

Benefactors

IT WILL NOT be amiss here to mention some of the benefactors who have rendered special help to the Carmel of
Allentown. The Very Reverend Lawrence C. Diether,
O. Carm., of Chicago, contributed towards the novitiate
wing, and stood security for the indebtedness of the
buildings to be erected. His interest in the Allentown
Carmel knew no bounds, and if this zealous Provincial
had lived, his one desire was to be permanent Chaplain
in Saint Therese's Valley. In fact, a most marvelous
feature in the construction of the new Carmel, was the
immediate and liberal response of priests, religious and
lay benefactors.

Mr. Matthew H. McCloskey, Jr., of Philadelphia,
created a Chamberlain of Sword and Cape by His Holiness, Pope Pius XII, proved a friend in need. His devotedness to Saint Therese prompted his interest in the
Little Flower Carmel at Allentown. Due to the great
liberality of Miss Ethel B. Waters, through the years,
the Carmelites were able to install an immense drainage
system, and also a heating unit in one of the buildings.
Mr. John D. Fuller, of Bedford, Indiana, a convert to

the Catholic Church, provided the limestone for the trimming of the Monastery buildings, as well as for the Chapel-façade, together with the eight-foot statue of Saint Therese which enhances the splendid symmetry of the main entrance, and embellishes the harmonious simplicity of the façade. Mr. Bernard J. Schulte, a life-long friend of the Foundress, was among the very first benefactors.

Constantly assisting the work of the Carmelites, were the numerous friends and devotees of the Little Flower of Jesus, whose humble offerings proved the mainstay and unfailing support in the building of the Carmel of Allentown. It would be impossible to list each friend and benefactor; let it suffice that their good deeds evoke the unceasing prayers of the cloistered nuns of Carmel. Mention goes out to the following whose special help and services proved a giant factor in the cause of Carmel: Miss Angela Catalane, Mrs. Alfred B. Wade, Miss Catherine F. Cahill, Mrs. John L. Lanshe, Mr. Stephen Soltis, Mr. Paul S. Spaar, Mrs. Charles Daut, Mr. Vincent Messina, Mr. John Gulla, Mr. Michael Kaiser. Among Religious benefactors was the foundress of the Carmelite Sisters for the Aged and Infirm, the Reverend Mother M. Angeline Teresa, O. Carm., Superior General.

Mother Angeline Teresa's limitless kindness and interest in the Allentown Carmel, were a source of

· encouragement and help to the young community. And, remarkable to relate, her own great work of establishing a Religious Institute commenced about the same time as the Allentown foundation began, and like its Sister-Carmel, under the Divine Dew of God's Blessing, continues to prosper. Mother Angeline Teresa enjoyed the intimate friendship of the two foundresses.

Outstanding among the Priest-benefactors were the Reverend Theodore Maria Roessler, of Belfield, North Dakota, and the Right Reverend Monsignor Florence J. Halloran, V.F., of Wakefield, Massachusetts.

Monsignor Halloran showed a lively and paternal interest in the spiritual and temporal growth of the Carmel of Allentown, and maintained an edifying correspondence with the foundresses, until his holy death on March 27, 1947. Prior to this time, he went so far as to arrange for a gift to be used for a future foundation of Carmel, to branch out from the Monastery at Allentown, in honor of his beloved friend, the "Little Flower" —Saint Therese of the Child Jesus, to whom he was ardently devoted. Also, as mentioned heretofore, Father Hammeke remained a loyal and kind friend through the years.

But a most important link in our history would be missing were we to omit that the real founder and the very first benefactor of the new Carmel was the zealous Priest-uncle of Mother Therese, the Reverend Father

Albert M. Horck, of Oregon, whose legacy to his niece, was intended to provide for the expansion of Carmel.

THE MONASTERY GARDEN

Tilling the soil in the Monastery Garden, Little Flower Carmel, Allentown, Pa.

THE NOVITIATE WING AND BELL TOWER

Novitiate Wing and Bell Tower, Carmel of the Little Flower, Allentown, Pa.

CHAPTER TWENTY-TWO

Shrine-Chapel of Saint Therese

ON DECEMBER 8, 1934, Feast of the Immaculate Conception, the little group of Carmelite Sisters, with picks
and shovels, commenced the excavation for the building
of the Chapel. They persevered in their hard labors and
were most industrious so that by March 19, of the
following year, the Feast of Saint Joseph, Protector of
the Carmelite Order, the masons were able to commence
the stone work. It was to be a majestic stone edifice of
Roman style. Mother Therese early formulated the idea
to have the Chapel and Monastery buildings a close
duplicate of the Chapel and Carmel of Lisieux.

CORNERSTONE-LAYING

It was likewise on the great Feast of the Immaculate
Conception, 1935 that the Auxiliary Bishop of Philadelphia, the Most Reverend Gerald P. O'Hara, D.D.,
J.U.D., laid the cornerstone before an immense throng
of friends of the Carmelites. In addition to His Excel-
lency, the Bishop, there were present on this memorable
occasion: the Right Reverend Monsignor Leo G. Fink,
V.F.; the Very Reverend Lawrence C. Diether, O.

145

Carm., of Chicago; the Very Reverend Silverius J. Quigley, O. Carm., of Englewood; the Reverend Urban Lager, O. Carm., of Chicago; the Reverend Peter Kramer, O. Carm., of Leonia; the Reverend Joseph L. Mathis, of Allentown; and the Reverend Joseph Kavanagh, secretary to Bishop O'Hara. Father Quigley preached the sermon.

Outside Shrine

Gracing the spacious side-entrance of the chapel is an immense life-like statue of Saint Therese as the Patroness of the Missions. Four angels, carved in stone, adorn four prominent piers.

Main Altar

The beautiful main altar of exquisite Carrara marble was presented to the Carmelite nuns by the Reverend Father William Hammeke and his parishioners from St. Paul's, Reading.

Towering over the main altar is the lovely shrine-group, depicting Saint Therese showering her roses from Heaven, close to the Immaculate Queen of Carmel, and her Divine Child. This marble group is an elaborate and truly devotional piece of art.

Iron Grille

To the left of the Sanctuary, an immense grille of iron separates the cloister from the public. This grille was the gift of Mrs. Martin Roessler, of California, given in memory of her late husband, the uncle of Sister Clement Mary.

THE CUPOLA

An outstanding copper cupola towers majestically over the Sanctuary, and can be seen for miles away. The erection of this grand cupola was made possible through the extreme kindness of Miss Ethel B. Waters.

SIDE ALTARS

The two side altars came from Saint Stephen's Church, in Shenandoah. The delicately beautiful shrine of Our Lady of Mount Carmel is enthroned on the one side. And a most impressive statue of Saint Joseph, Patron and Protector of the Carmelites, holds a prominent place on the opposite side. The other spaces contain shrines of the Sacred Heart, of the Miraculous Infant Jesus of Prague, of Saint Anne, of Saint Jude, and of Saint Philomena, the wonder-worker and special advocate of the Cure of Ars. The great mystics of Carmel, Saint Teresa of Avila, and Saint John of the Cross, also, have their special places in the new Chapel. The gifts of these shrines were presented to the Carmel by devoted friends.

Pipe-Organ

Behind the large, iron grille, over the choir, is a balcony. Here was installed an Estey organ of splendid tone, which greatly enhances the spiritual atmosphere of the surroundings. Mr. Matthew H. McCloskey, Jr., gave this welcome gift to Carmel.

Stained Glass Windows

Mother Therese likewise planned the theme that should be depicted in each window of stained glass. All the windows on the Gospel side reproduced scenes from the life of Saint Therese of the Child Jesus, the Patroness of the Chapel: first, Saint Therese as a novice, standing at the foot of the Calvary, in the courtyard of the Carmel; second, on the evening of her Profession, communing with God, she contemplates the starry heavens; third, as Sacristan, she prepares the Sacred Vessels for the Holy Sacrifice of the Mass; fourth, lying in state after death, her angelic countenance continues to reflect her last ecstasy of consuming love; fifth, the Saint in glory, showers her promised roses upon the earth . . . , upon souls!

Saint Teresa of Avila Window

On the opposite side, over the entrance, is a window dedicated to the seraphic Mother, Saint Teresa of Avila,

Impressive Side View
Carmelite Monastery, Allentown, Pa.

View of Public Chapel of the
Convent Showing People As-
sembled for a Profession
Ceremony

Main Altar of Cararra Marble,
Little Flower Chapel, Carmelite
Monastery, Allentown, Pa.

reproducing an episode in her life. Christ appeared to her in the cloister of Carmel, in the form of a little child, with wondrous countenance and flowing hair. Teresa, amazed at the celestial visitor, deigned to inquire: "And who art thou?"

He answered her softly: "Tell me first what thou art called."

"Teresa of Jesus is my name." And His gentle answer sweetly told her: "And I am Jesus of Teresa . . . "

Facing the street side, the massive windows represent the following: Our Lady of Mount Carmel, assisting the children of Carmel, detained in Purgatory, speedily releases the wearers of Her Brown Scapular, especially on the first Saturday after death. The second window depicts Saint Elias, the great Prophet of Carmel, ascending into the heavens by a whirlwind which had assumed the form of a fiery chariot. The third window shows the Patrons of the Carmelite Order, representing the Miraculous Infant Jesus of Prague, surrounded by a host of Carmelite Saints. The theme of the fourth window is Saint Therese of the Child Jesus, receiving her First Holy Communion, whose entranced face reveals her inward rapture on this first visit of Jesus to her soul; and the fifth window represents the Little Flower, receiving the Holy Habit of Carmel, when she kneels before the enclosure door to receive her father's blessing.

"The Queen of Heaven to her little Mary" is the title of a poem composed by Saint Therese. The symbolic representation shows Our Dear Lady with the Child Jesus and Little Therese. The enchanting thought is that Therese, possessing a childlike spirit, resembles the Little Christ, and is worthy to be cradled with Him, upon the bosom of Holy Mary.

The second window depicts Saint Therese, "mystically wounded by Divine Love"; it shows the Saint making the Way of the Cross, when she felt herself wounded by a dart of fire, so ardent, that she thought she would die; third, in the garden at Carmel, she contemplates the Sacred Heart, and pictures her soul as a little dove in exile, longing for the moment when it may fly to the Divine Ark of the Heart of Christ; fourth, on her death-bed, in an ecstasy of love, she sings her last love-song on earth: "My God, I love Thee"; and fifth, as patroness of the Missions, she is seen coming down from heaven, to scatter her roses of grace, and of blessing, upon the missions of Mother Church, throughout the world.

FACADE WINDOWS

With the erection of the Chapel-façade, two massive stained glass windows, and a large oval one, were added to the sacred edifice: the first one depicts the seraphic virgin of Carmel, Saint Mary Magdalen di Pazzi, the special Patroness of the Monastery; in the second, we behold the powerful Protector of the Universal Church, Saint Michael, the Archangel; and the large oval window, directly over the main entrance, is dedicated to Christ, Our Lord, as the "Agnus Dei."

CONTINUED PROGRESS

The Community, without doubt, had many struggles during those trying times. Living elbow to elbow, in cramped quarters while the building was going up, provided salutary means of penance, mortification, and real hardship. But the prayers never ceased, and Our Lord, always lavish and merciful to the trustful, was ever ready with His comforting rewards. People, too, were always generous and sympathetic with the nuns. They saw to it that the Sisters had sufficient food, and other necessities.

There were times, of course, when some item, much needed, was lacking. And then, at the very last moment, some good Samaritan would appear who provided relief in the needed cause. This was inevitably the case, and so much so, that it seemed our Blessed Lord would not allow His spouses to go to the end of their strength, or to sound the depths of their blind confidence in His ever-loving Providence.

151

Catholics and non-Catholics offered their labor, provisions and donations to the noble cause. But it must be admitted that no one could refuse Mother Therese; she had only to hint at something, and it would be immediately forthcoming. Indeed some of the stories in this connection provide much merriment. On one occasion a Jewish friend was brought to the Monastery on some business. He had heard of the "saintly" Mother Therese, and he wished also to meet her. It did not take him long to recognize a great business executive in the little nun before him, still he hesitated and wavered . . . before he presented his alms. Afterwards he gave Mother Therese an offering, remarking naively: "Mother, you are a regular Jew."

Now, with the novitiate wing a reality, the crypt constructed, and the Chapel ready to use, Mother Therese's desire was to complete the quadrangle, and, later on, the façade. She was not given to wasting time, but, together with her devoted nuns, and a few volunteers, began the foundation of the Convent proper. Thus the unfinished Chapel-front formed the north wall of the quadrangle, the novitiate wing the east wall, the professed nuns' wing would form the south wall, and the speak-room section and part of the Chapel would form the west wall.

Day after day, the Sisters toiled laboriously, but joyfully, in the dear Lord's vineyard, so that by the Fall of

1938, much of the overcrowded condition was relieved by occupying the new cells in the south wing. The last portions of the building that remained unfinished were the northeast corner where the bell-tower was to be erected, and the main entrance to the Chapel with façade. Everything else was in order! Even the great stone Crucifix, called "the Calvary" had already been placed in the center of the quadrangle, enhancing the tastefully-laid-out courtyard, which seemed to take on a radiant aspect, reflecting the serene loveliness of a hidden paradise.

THIRD ORDER CENTRE FOR LAITY

Not content with guiding her little community in the mystical life of prayer and contemplation, and to form them "to meditate day and night on the law of the Lord," as the Holy Rule of Carmel prescribes (Chapter VII), Mother Therese like the Prophets and Doctors of Mother Church, became a light unto souls. She wished ardently to draw all souls to the interior life, and to a deeper appreciation of true spirituality. Likewise she strove unceasingly to impress upon others the real meaning of the sacrificial life of Carmel, and the proper explanation of the cloister-vocation.

So it was a source of special joy to her to assist in the establishment of a Third Order Centre, for the laity, who would wish to become tertiaries of Our Lady of

Mount Carmel, and wearers of Her Brown Scapular, honoring the Queen of Carmel by the purity of their lives and their spirit of prayerfulness amidst the turmoil of the world.

The Provincial of the Carmelites, the Very Reverend Matthew T. O'Neill, O. Carm., arranged for the inauguration of the Third Order, delegating Father Anthony, O. Carm., of Pittsburgh, to conduct the first reception on the Scapular Feast, July 16, 1937, on which occasion sixty men and women joined the ranks of the tertiaries. Remarkable to relate, in less than two years from this date, the membership increased to two hundred.

"Now that she is in heaven, she will help Saint Therese to shower roses on earth . . ."

Carmelites of Lisieux

PART IV

"Veni, Sponsa Christi!"

"Arise, my love . . . and come! Make haste, my love, my dove, my beautiful one, and come! The winter (of exile) is now past, the storms (of life) are over, the sweet sun of love again shines forth in a delightful spring. Come, show me thy face, and let us speak again of love, that I may unite Myself to thee, with eternal bonds, the bonds of Divine Bethrothal, and of Mystical Nuptials."

Cloister—Quadrangle, showing "The Calvary," Carmelite Monastery, Saint Therese's Valley, Allentown, Pa.

Nuns in procession in the Garden of Carmel, Carmelite Monastery, Allentown, Pa.

CHAPTER TWENTY-THREE

"Veni, Sponsa Christi"
("Come, Spouse of Christ")

IT WAS Holy Week, in April, of 1939. The increased spiritual functions necessitated freedom from all that was not absolutely necessary to be done. And in the calm, silent atmosphere of the cloister, Mother Therese was better able to apply herself at this time to the un-ceasing mental work, and to the Easter correspondence, which she continued to do at night, since this work was not to be laid aside.

It was the evening of Holy Thursday. Twilight hovered over the serene valley. The refreshing quietude that reigned within the Carmel, filled the soul with a restful peace. Mother Therese was about to give to her community one of the most beautiful lessons we find exemplified in the very life of our dear Master Himself, which He enacted on the eve of His sad departure from His Apostles. Was no one aware of the not-too-distant murmur of another farewell that was to follow shortly?

Fulfilling the sacred custom of Maundy Thursday, Mother Therese, with a white towel shielding her holy Scapular, proceeded with her humble task. Kneeling before her daughters, she washed their feet, then, inclining to the floor, she pressed her lips to the foot of each. This constant bending over, this great exertion, surely must have intensified the pain that was already afflicting her generous heart, but she suffered in silence!

Later in the same evening, on reaching her office-room, the cheery greeting of her "little secretary" brought a smile to her lips. At the same moment, however, involuntarily, she pressed her hand to her heart, as if to relieve a pressure, and she gasped for breath. "You shouldn't have gone through with that long exercise, Mother. It was too much for you," remonstrated her secretary. Mother Therese seemed to smile at the tender admonition, and seating herself before her desk, she responded simply: "It had to be done." Before her "little helper" could say anything else, Mother's tone became even gay as she remarked, in her unfailing humor: "But I saw all kinds of feet to-day, Sister!"

Afterwards, whilst preparing Easter "souvenirs" for the friends of the community, the saintly Mother expressed herself thus: "The Divine Office is so beautiful. I so love to chant it. I could sing all the Lessons myself."

On the eve of Good Friday, the nuns took turns, hour by hour, to pray at the Sepulchre of Our Lord in the Chapel. It was a cold, damp night. Mother Therese, kneeling alone in the pew, kept her vigil from nine to ten o'clock, in the evening. The chilly atmosphere was not at all inviting, and she surely must have felt it, although she seemed to take no notice of it. Indeed, in every circumstance, she sought, first and foremost, the Presence of God.

Her peaceful, prayerful mien mirrored this truth, that she had mastered the art of intimacy with the Master. It was the very essence of her interior life, and she never left off practicing this mystical doctrine, so characteristic of Carmelite spirituality. It was inspiring to look upon her kneeling figure. There was always something very irresistible about Mother Therese. Especially, when she was immersed in prayer, united to her Suffering Saviour, or contemplating her King in the Blessed Sacrament, one felt it difficult to withdraw one's eyes from her celestial countenance. Her love for the Holy Rosary of the Mother of God and for the Way of the Cross was profound and these two exercises of piety were paramount devotions throughout her whole life. And she was especially devoted to Saint Joseph.

"After a half hour, I was becoming a little restless in the cold Chapel," relates one of the nuns, who was present on that same Good Friday eve. "And I cast my gaze more and more upon our Mother. The flickering candle-light showed me her face, pale and tired, the lips moving in prayer. Her eyes were fixed upon the Tabernacle. I continued to look upon her; and I couldn't help saying to myself (as Little Therese said of her venerable father): 'when I look at her, I know how the saints prayed!' "

Was this, then, the hour when she offered to Him, her humble Fiat, or, was her prayer, like His own: "Father, not my will, but Thine be done"? Only God knew this; and that was enough!

Mother Therese performed each and every exercise of that last Holy Week, as always, with edifying fervor and exactness. She simply went on—self was forgotten despite the increased bodily pains. On Holy Saturday, after the long services in the Chapel, taking the Easter Water, Mother Therese, together with her Assistant, journeyed from building to building, blessing the cells, the rooms, and every department of the Monastery. Surely all this must have caused the poor sufferer over-whelming fatigue.

Mother Therese looked for no earthly reward for her incessant labors. She labored for GOD. Everything else was passing. And, she labored in peace! She seemed to consider herself a mere "nothing," God's poor, little handmaid, and so, He Alone, sufficed for her. *He* would be her Reward.

> "Thou art my champion and my refuge; do not linger, my God, do not linger on the way."
>
> (Ps. 39, 18.)

Easter Sunday dawned! It would have been a great joy to Mother to be able to spend the day with her dear nuns. But sacrifice is never to be laid aside. Affairs, inside and outside of the house, compelled her to "keep on the go," even on the great Feast of Easter. And this, despite the fact that she was really on the point of complete exhaustion.

On Easter Monday she prepared the coffee for the Sisters' breakfast. This was a part of her daily "ritual." The conventual Mass was as usual at seven o'clock. After the Holy Sacrifice, she had a slight heart attack. This did not prevent Mother from making her Thanksgiving after Holy Communion, and so, she retired to a little room, next to the choir, and remained, seated in a chair, to finish her prayers, and to regain her strength. In a short time, she resumed her duties. The nuns remonstrated with her, lovingly, and with filial affection, saying: "You ought to rest, dear Mother." And on this day, she replied, almost prophetically: "Tomorrow, I will rest all day." And really, as she had foretold, it was on the following day that she entered into Eternal Rest.

On that memorable morning, she was almost too ill to rise for the Community exercises. In fact, an acute attack of pain in her chest made it difficult for her even to move from her bed. One of the nuns feelingly tried to persuade her to remain in bed, and not to come to the choir for Mass. The intrepid Mother, valiant and self-effacing to the last, seemed quite taken back at the mere hint of such a deprivation. Without hesitation, gently,

161

but with a firm conviction, she replied simply: "Sister, I would not miss Holy Communion for anything in the world." Having faithfully concurred with the Divine during the course of her entire life, in these last remaining hours she would depend directly on her unfailing Lord. Ah, she too, like Saint Mary Magdalen di Pazzi, and the intimate friends of the Saviour, hungered after Holy Communion.

Death of Mother Therese

"As the hart panteth after the fountains of water,
so doth my soul pant after Thee, O my God."

(Ps. 41.)

Guided unceasingly by the valiant maxim, which she strove faithfully to follow for her own soul's sanctification, Mother Therese practiced self-forgetfulness so completely that she hardly realized her poor, frail body was utterly worn out, under the constant strain of her endless spiritual and material labors. Moreover she had undergone two major operations shortly after the founding of the new Carmel, each of which had brought her to the very threshold of eternity. It was her "intimate friend," Saint Therese of the Child Jesus, who cured her after the second operation, when Mother Therese lay in a coma for three days, consumed by fever. The General of the Carmelites, the Most Reverend Father Elias Magennis, O. Carm., inspecting the American

Carmels, at the time, visited Mother Therese at the hospital, and took occasion to bless her with a First Class Relic of Saint Therese of the Child Jesus. Instantly, her fever subsided, and she experienced a return of strength and of life. She was profoundly grateful to God, and to His "Little Therese," for this favor. Nevertheless, it was an effort for her, as she herself told afterwards, to return to life after her consoling proximity to Life Eternal.

It was as though His dear persuasion, gently but forcibly, increased her hunger and thirst for the Beloved of her soul! The "dove" in exile, sighed continually for its Divine Mate, in Paradise, and she would not be wholly at rest, nor would her sweet yearnings abate, until, in His Dear Presence, she would be safe and at rest in the very Heart of Eternal Love. The magnanimous soul of the humble Foundress would fly to its True Home! And, indeed, Mother Therese gave her very life for the new Carmel.

"Ecce, venio!"

On Easter Tuesday morning, April 11, 1939, at about ten-fifteen o'clock, barely three hours after Mother's reception of Holy Communion during the conventual Mass, a heart attack broke the frail ties that bound to earth this zealous spouse of the Most Blessed Trinity. Her death was hastened, perhaps, by her untiring zeal in the holy service of her Lord and Master, Whose greater honor and glory were the mainspring of her entire spiritual life.

Wise virgin that she was, she kept her lamp trimmed . . . Her Mystical Bridegroom, as the Divine Eagle, swooped down into the little room that served as her office and her humble cell, and bore her blessed, merit-laden soul to the realms of the Heavenly Carmel. A moment before, sitting at her desk, she had fixed her gaze on a picture of our cherished Saint Therese, which hung over her bed. During that gaze of love, she went Home!

Her faithful "Guardian Angel" and her "little secretary" were with her at this supreme moment. She, whose motto was: "Souls for Jesus and Mary through Little Therese," was greeted, we may believe, at the threshold of Eternity, by her loving and intimate friend, the "Little Flower" of Jesus and Mary.

After her gentle passing, her body remained so supple, and so life-like, that it appeared that she had merely fallen asleep. A soft smile played about the lips, and her dear countenance, just as in life, radiated peace and rest. However, her "little secretary" noticing a single tear glistening on the eyelid, took a linen handkerchief, and tenderly preserved the "sparkling gem." Now the Sisters of Carmel have the happiness of possessing their saintly Mother's last tear.

Loving hands placed the dear body in the casket prepared for her, and she lay in state, behind the cloister-
grille, in the Monastery choir, facing the Main Altar.
Hundreds of friends and benefactors, men, women, children, priests, and religious, filed past the grille window
to pay a last farewell to Mother Therese. Without any
ado, those who knew her during life, were inspired to
pass through the grating rosaries, crosses, medals, pictures, and other items, to be touched to her venerable
body, that they might be kept by them as precious
"souvenirs."

Funeral and Obsequies

The final obsequies for the beloved Foundress of the
Carmel of Allentown, were held on Friday morning,
April 14, at ten o'clock, in the Monastery Chapel. A
Solemn High Mass of Requiem was celebrated by the
Very Reverend Silverius J. Quigley, O. Carm., while
Rev. Henry Goodwin, O. Carm., was Deacon, and Rev.
Wilfrid Smith, O. Carm., was Sub-Deacon. The boys'
Gregorian choir from Sacred Heart Church, Allentown,
sang the Mass. Rev. Anthony Dressel, O. Carm.,
preached the eulogy. The Very Reverend Lawrence D.
Flanagan, O. Carm., performed the Absolution cere-
monial.

Previous to the celebration of the Solemn High Mass,
the Divine Office was recited by the attending Clergy,

in the Sanctuary. The Right Reverend Monsignor Leo G. Fink, V.F., presided at the recitation of the Divine Office and at the Solemn Mass. Among the secular Clergy were priests from Allentown, Reading, Bethlehem and vicinity

The burial rites concluded, the nuns of the community acted as pallbearers, carrying the body of their venerable Mother and Foundress, to the mausoleum Chapel, in the Monastery garden, where the interment took place. Here the casket was hermetically sealed in the vault prepared for Mother Therese, beside the votive Altar. The Benedictus was chanted and prayers for the spiritual repose of her soul were offered by the Carmelites. The Very Reverend Matthew T. O'Neill, O. Carm., Provincial, pronounced the Last Absolution as the tomb was sealed.

CHAPTER TWENTY-FOUR

Tributes of Devotion

CARDINAL DOUGHERTY SENDS CONDOLENCE

IN A LETTER of April 23, 1939, addressed to Mother Clement Mary, His Eminence, the Most Reverend Archbishop, Dennis Cardinal Dougherty, of Philadelphia, expressed his sympathy in the death of the Reverend Mother Therese of Jesus:

"As it was a shock to you, it was also a shock to me to learn how suddenly she was called, but it is a consolation to her late children, and to myself, that she was ever prepared for the call. She has left behind her a monument in the erection of your Monastery, but still more, in the religious formation which she gave to her Community. She, as well as yourselves, will be remembered by me in Masses and prayers."

FROM THE PRIOR GENERAL OF THE CARMELITES

We quote from the letter of the Most Reverend Father Kilian E. Lynch, Prior General, Ord. Carm., sent to the Allentown Carmel on the Feast of Saint Elias, July 20, 1948:

" . . . It was with the greatest interest that I read the life of your Foundress whom I had the privilege of meeting when your Carmel was only in its infancy. When I re-visited Allentown a few days ago, I was amazed to see what she accomplished in the span of a few years. Every stone of your imposing monastery seems to give testimony to the zeal and heroic self-sacrifice of its Foundress. It was surely the hand of God that led her to Saint Therese's Valley and had His grace not supported her she could never have overcome all the obstacles that stood in her way.

"However, the real monument to Mother Therese is not in stone but in the spirit of prayer and union with God which she has bequeathed to her community as her most precious heritage.

"May she protect you from Heaven and be your constant intercessor before the throne of grace until you are one with her in the glorious Carmel of eternity."

From the Carmelites of Lisieux

The living sister of Saint Therese of the Child Jesus, the Reverend Mother Agnes of Jesus, Prioress of the Lisieux Carmel, wrote as follows, on July 3, 1939:

"It was indeed a great shock to hear of Reverend Mother Therese of Jesus' death. When she wrote in April, she seemed so full of life! God called her quickly but she was ready to say "Adsum." Now that she is in

168

Heaven, she will help Saint Therese to shower roses on earth, and on whom will she let them fall if not on the dear Monastery which she founded, and for which she worked so much. We are sure that you already feel her protection.

"Saint Therese of the Child Jesus cannot forget all that the dear departed one did to make her known, and she (Saint Therese) must have been there, at the last moment, to introduce the dear soul in Heaven.

"What a glorious welcome she must have had above!

"Many thanks for the two photos enclosed in your letter. How kind dear Mother Therese of Jesus appears! She seems to be kindness and mildness personified."

From a Correspondent

Writing to the Sisters, on August 9, 1947, Mrs. Alfred B. Wade, of New Canaan, Connecticut, eulogized Mother Therese:

"I made the acquaintance of Mother Therese of Jesus through an appeal of hers for their desperately poor Convent in Naples, which was published in *The Commonweal*. That started a correspondence which lasted until the end of her life, and which was an unfailing source of inspiration, and comfort, during a very trying period.

"Not too long after the appeal appeared in *The Commonweal*, she was authorized by her Superiors to

make a new foundation in the United States. With unfailing courage, she undertook the seemingly impossible
task of building a new Carmel, with no great material
backing, but like all God's work, it, of course, succeeded,
and she lived to see the result of the labor and hardships
she had endured to achieve that goal.

"No one who had the privilege of knowing her—
(even by correspondence as in my case) could fail to be
impressed with her *never-failing confidence* in *God's
help,* her personal courage, and her Christ-like sympathy
for the trials and anxieties of others. Her sympathy was
never tiring—she was a Christ-like person."

FROM THE CARMELITES OF ROME

Writing to his spiritual Sister, on May 6, 1939, the
zealous Carmelite, Father Clement Mary, wrote as
follows:

"To-day I send you my message, after receiving from
you the unexpected and sad notification of the sudden
death of our highly-esteemed and unforgettable Mother
Therese.

"Please accept, dear Mother, my dearest and sincerest
condolence upon this great loss to you and to your
deeply-grieved Community.

"I know quite well what Mother Therese has done,
offered, and suffered for the foundation of Carmel at
Allentown. But, indeed, behold what she—has accom-

plished, through the grace of God, in these few years, is simply marvelous. In a short time, she brought to flower a new, richly-blooming garden of Carmel.

"Mother Therese—blessed and happy—has surely received a richly-deserved reward in Heaven.

"I myself at least do not doubt about it; and you, good Mother, know very well that I have always known her good and holy desires.

"Mother Therese . . . is never forgotten by the Carmelites in Rome, nor is she forgotten by the Sisters in the "Regina Coeli" Carmel . . . (formerly the Carmel of Saint Bridget)."

MESSAGE OF A BENEFACTRESS

Mrs. Marie Potter Froelich, of Bethlehem, Pennsylvania, friend and benefactress of the Carmel, through the years, sent the following message to the Community in Saint Therese's Valley:

" . . . Your Carmelite Monastery was brought to my attention during the first year of founding in 1931, by the act of a friend whose simple words: 'the nuns need you,' let fall the missionary seed of spiritual propagation.

"Reflecting at the close of 1947, my eyes wander over the Valley of Saint Therese, shrouded in a blanket of white, and mentally, once more I kneel with the throng of worshippers, gathered for the first Mass on Christmas of 1931, held in the residence or first home of the venerable Foundress, Mother Therese, and her valiant band of Little Sisters of Carmel.

"The courtyard was filled with devout visitors, as the improvised chapel in the former living-room held but meagre accommodation, with the limited number of pews. A small white Altar held the Divine Presence, while the King of Kings reposed in a crib so humble. There, in an open stair-landing, stood the beautiful shrine-statue of Our Lady of Carmel, and lovely Therese, "the Little Flower."

"A glazed porch, quite inadequate against the rigor of winter, served the nuns as a choir. As their voices chanted this first Christmas Mass, could any missionary heart be aught but diffused with the warming elation of benediction.

"Upon a succeeding visit to the Chapel, I beheld Reverend Mother Therese of Jesus, alone, in deep and prayerful concentration. The choir had dispersed but our beloved Mother Therese prayed in an ecstasy of beatific radiance such as I never before beheld on any human face. Even after, I knew when I clasped my dear Friend's hand, that the touch of a sainted soul blessed my poor unworthy self.

"Many signal and remarkable benefits have been received by me since the beloved Foundress, Mother Therese of Jesus, has gone to her reward in 1939. I was the recipient of the promise she made during her saintly lifetime, that we, her patrons, would merit her first concern at the Throne of our dear Saviour."

From a Carmelite Father

The Very Reverend Father Arnold H. McCarthy, O. Carm., a former Definitor of the Carmelite Province of the Most Pure Heart of Mary, Chicago, Illinois, penned the following message in praise of the venerable Foundress of the Carmel of Allentown:

"All of Carmel's glory is not in the past. Nor is it all in the old world. Truly spiritual Bishops have always recognized the boundless spiritual wealth that an active diocese enjoys when it has within its boundaries contemplative convents, where cloistered women pray day and night for souls. The work of the old Carmels in the old world is carried on in the younger Carmels of the New World. God in His own way can make of little things mighty things.

"He was doing just that when He led Mother Therese of Jesus with one companion, Sister Clement Mary to bring the first Carmel of Nuns of the Ancient Observance, to Allentown, Pennsylvania.

"To have known Mother Therese of Jesus was to have known that there is really no transition from youth to old age as far as the spirit of Carmel is concerned. To have climbed over the rough planks and narrow catwalks of the half-finished convent that she and the nuns were building in a great measure with their own hands, and see this remarkable woman well on in years stepping more nimbly across the then uncloistered walls, than the writer who at the time had only been ordained a few years and considered himself quite limber, was to have etched into one's memory a picture that time has not been able to dull or erase.

"There was something so startingly alert and alive about this courageous little nun, and at the same time something so charmingly ancient and wise about her childlike cheerfulness and deep faith, that something cried out in your soul that, 'here is a woman who knows her God and whose God knows her.' It was she who set herself to the seemingly overwhelming task of keeping old Carmel ever young. Nothing seemed to daunt her. She was the sort of person you would almost expect to go to an empty cupboard and return with her arms laden with bread. Not that she was a dreamy-eyed visionary who expected God to do His own work and hers too. One visit with her would have dispelled any idea of that kind at once. Rather she was the embodiment of the traditional Carmelite who *prays* as if everything depended on God and *works* as if everything depended on her. Yet with all her activity, and it was great indeed, somehow you knew that she was never far from her cell, where as a Carmelite, obeying her ancient Rule remaining always if not physically, then really and truly there in spirit, 'meditating day and night on the law of the Lord.' For her there was no break-off between work and prayer, they both flowed into each other for her work was a prayer and prayer her life's work.

"Around this Mother gathered young souls who under her guidance and example were to form the first Carmel of the Ancient Observance for cloistered Carmelite nuns in our beloved Country."

From Her Intimate Friend

We quote from letters sent to the Community by Miss Marguerite Muehlenkamp, of Athens, Wisconsin, for many years the intimate friend of Mother Therese.

"Your sad message regarding the passing of our dearly loved and highly esteemed Mother Therese was a severe shock to me, in particular, as it came as the next word to a cheerful and loving letter from her at Easter time. Although my loss is great indeed, I feel that yours is immeasurably greater.

"You will sorely miss her motherly solicitude; her unfeigned piety; her unshakable faith and trust in Divine Providence; her executive ability, etc. All these and more that one might wish for in a superior.

"I am confident that she has not lost interest in you and in everything that relates to her heart's fondest desire—her holy foundation, and that, as she looks down from heaven upon you, is pleading your cause at the Throne of the Sacred Heart.

"As for myself, her memory shall always be a bene-diction, and I shall never cease thanking our dear Lord for all that she meant to me.

". . . My acquaintance with Mother Therese dates back in 1909, when my Reverend brother and I were spending some time in the West, for the recovery of his lost health.

"My Reverend brother said his daily Mass at Saint Louis, in a parish presided over by the Reverend Father Horck, the uncle of Mother Therese. Both were very kind to us.

"From our first meeting, Anna and I liked each other and had a high regard for each other which developed into a life-long friendship.

". . . I know that she was very happy and contented after entering Carmel! I still have a package of her letters, all of which breathe the spirit of profound piety.

"In all probability, you, dear Mother, who have been her confident and assistant for so many years, are more familiar with her subsequent years of trials, of her harassing disappointments, etc., than I would presume to portray.

"You have had abundant proof of her courage, forti-tude, and indomitable spirit, and later, of her holy joy and gratefulness, when finally settled in her own little Carmel . . .

"I shall send you her letters if you think they might be of help to you."

FROM A CONVERT

Mrs. John L. Eisenhard, of Topton, Pennsylvania, penned the following tribute to Mother Therese of Jesus, on June 12, 1948:

"It is a rare privilege and honor to pay tribute to the memory of Mother Therese.

"After the nuns had arrived at Lanark Manor, I accepted their invitation to visit the Convent. I went there from a curious angle rather than from any religious motive, as I did not belong to their Faith.

"From the moment I met Mother Therese of Jesus, I was impressed with her gracious personality, her simplicity and humaneness, and her deep religious love.

"I can recall vividly during the time that the new building was in progress, how I walked at her side in the Convent; the many times I conversed with her at the grille; the unforgettable Christmas Eve in the moonlit garden which she planned should one day become a replica of the one at Lisieux; her inspirational conversations about God, the Blessed Mother and the Saints; standing with her at the Altar; the anguish of seeing her suffer with a heart attack; the last time when she lay quiet (so peaceful and still), yet I am certain so very happy.

"My one great regret is that she was not living when I entered the Church of her Faith, but I am quite sure she knows, for I believe it was she who asked the Little Flower of Jesus to drop the rose-petals which tempered my illness during these later years—truly a great woman, a great Carmelite Sister and a Saint."

From Her Grateful Community

"Dear little Mother, you are not gone from us. We feel your blessed presence everywhere; in every nook and corner of the dear Monastery which you designed with such extreme insight, wisdom and loving care.

"Day after day, fulfilling our sacred duties, we slip away to visit at your tomb. Loving hands and grateful hearts keep flowers there—the flowers you so loved! Prayers ascend heavenwards. And as we kneel, we find ourselves praying *to* you,—telling you of our gratitude for all you have done for us, of what we need to continue in the way first tread by your dear steps, and imploring help, just as we were wont to do when we knocked at your cell-door, and found you always patient, always willing to listen to us.

"You are not gone from us! Your kindly spirit abides in the dear Community. How could we forget you, your ever-present smile of grace, your gracious words, your unfailing encouragement! How you loved, and suffered! How many beautiful lessons you taught and exemplified for your devoted children in Carmel! You so clearly reflected, by your holy life, the impelling maxim of Saint Paul: 'I live, now not I, but *Christ* liveth in me.'

"O little Mother, continue from on High to be our "Kindly light," now that you are immersed in the Light of Eternal Radiance. And you know *now* His exquisite, indescribable Peace, in the glory of the Light of God.

"Our own little Mother Therese, beloved Spouse of Jesus, pray for your grateful children of the Allentown Carmel!"

✶ ✶ ✶

The following verses were written by the "little secretary" of Mother Therese, in memory of the saintly Mother and Foundress of the Carmel of Allentown, on October 15, 1939, the anniversary of Mother's entrance into Carmel.

" 'Tis Our 'Remember Thou' "

Oh, dearest Mother:

Remember how these little rhymes
  Would cause your gentle face
To light in smiles, and all the while . . .
  Your soul was fixed in grace!

179

Remember all the little songs we sang,
That gave you joy;
And how tenderly you sang your song on Christmas
Eve,
To Mary's little Boy!

Remember what you said: "Oh, how I love to
chant . . .
The lamentations sad, at Eastertide."
Yet all the while, the Master's Hand was drawing
thee aside.
Remember, too, when in the garden wide,
We labored there;
In humble act, your own hands worked the ground,
And made the hardest task, so luminously fair!

Remember how you loved the flowers gay,
The lovely rose, the lily fair,
And hemlock trees, forget-me-nots, and evergreens:
Your favorites were!
The laundry was transformed into a garden bright.
Content and smiling was your gaze!
Already had He given:
A glimpse, to thee, of distant scene,
The call, that leads to Heaven?

Remember, too, the childish pranks we played?
And how you laughed, and, sometimes, chided, too,
   Lest we had strayed . . .
   Yet full of glee,
You loved the joyful heart, the happy face, and
   Sweet humility!

Remember, when the little chicks, you housed,
And gave them barley flour,
Crumbs of bread, and grounded wheat, and corn . . .
   Oh! they were happy hours.

Remember, when the Gander, getting "playful"—
Stretched his neck, and surged, to fight the "foe":
And your umbrella stick was quite a weapon—
   To set him "on his heels," and quickly go.

Remember how, on Holy Thursday night,
   Your vigil kept from nine to ten;
Ah, happy hour, with the Bridegroom, fair!
   Unveiled, His message brief—perhaps, e'en then?

Remember, too, your last sweet legacy—
   Two simple words: "Be good."
Ingratitude was mine; we failed to see,
   And e'en misunderstood
      God's love.

But then, we know the depths
Of your sweet Mother-heart:
    Fair model of His own!
From realms above, you'll teach our yearning souls,
    To thirst for Him Alone.

Unfading memories, these, in exile's short demesne.
    No greater Gift than this, could He have given:
In Holy Mass, from His own lips, sweet words,
    The Foundress is in Heaven!

✶ ✶ ✶

"Urgent Requests to the Divine Bridegroom"

The following letter of petitions was composed by
Reverend Mother Therese, and she certainly *never* intended it for publication. Having carefully preserved
the letter, her "Guardian Angel" had the privilege to
carry its petitions, upon her heart, on her Clothing Day,
for presentation to the Divine Bridegroom.

In Carmel, it is customary to write out intentions and
petitions, especially on the occasions of Clothing and
Profession Days. These petitions are subsequently presented to Our Lord by the new Bride of Christ, during
the solemn act of prostration, at the time of the Spiritual
Nuptials.

182

THE LETTER

"O Divine Bridegroom of my dear child and first spiritual daughter, — vouchsafe to grant her, to-day, as a bridal gift, those great graces for which we most tenderly beseech Thee:

"That we may secure a suitable dwelling for the Monastery.

"That only such souls may come who will be of one mind and one heart, nuns who will be imbued with a true love of God and of the neighbor; who will be faithful observers of the Holy Rule of Carmel, and of its Silence.

"Give us souls who will be eager to practice all the virtues that are consonant with our particular mode of life, and are required for the holy observance of our sacred Vows of Poverty, Chastity, and Obedience.

"O grant that we may please Thee, by living a saintly life,—for our own soul's sanctification, and for the privilege of saving countless souls for Thee.

"Through Thy merits, grant us a blessed death, and afterwards, the joy of arriving at the degree of glory which Thou hast prepared for each of us.

"Also, bestow upon our relatives, friends, benefactors, and upon all those who wish to be remembered in our prayers,—all the graces they desire, and need, for their Eternal Salvation.

"In Thy Love and Suffering, O JESUS, we both wish to live and die.

> "Your two little spouses,
>> Mother Therese, and
>> Sister — —

October 1, 1928.

Behold how each line of her letter diffuses a rich spiritual fragrance, nay rather, it is a beautiful unfolding of the fecundity of her profound Faith, her child-like Trust, and her total Dependence upon God. Is it not a limpid manifestation of the interior spirit of Mother Therese, who always, and at all times, sought only the greater honor and glory of God!

CHAPTER TWENTY-FIVE

Mother Therese—
A Channel for God's Favors

IF WE MAY judge by the letters that continue to arrive at the Carmel of Allentown, God seems pleased to answer favorably prayers addressed to Him, through the intercession of Mother Therese of Jesus.

It may be of interest to our readers, if we but note a few of these answers to prayers. We, of course, confine ourselves to a bare statement of the facts recorded, without pronouncing on their supernatural character, leaving Holy Mother Church to be sole judge in matters of such delicacy.

FROM ROCHESTER, NEW YORK

After having sought the prayers of the Carmelites at Allentown, in the time of critical pregnancy, Mrs. Thomas Scott, of Rochester, New York, was invited to address her petition to the Most Holy Trinity, through the intercession of Mother Therese of Jesus. She asked for and obtained a small piece of linen worn by the late Foundress. Then, on October 10, 1946, she wrote as follows to the Allentown Carmel:

"Thanks to the intercession of Mother Therese of Jesus, to the Holy Trinity, a 'miracle' has been granted. A boy, weighing 10 lbs. 1 oz. was born normally in record time of one and one-half hours of *complete labor*. Please arrange a public thanksgiving in any suitable form."

In her letter of June 16, 1947, Mrs. Scott wrote the following: "I am happy to enclose the statement from my doctor that you requested. He was most happy to oblige, although he is not a Catholic. Doctor McIntosh also gives his permission to use his name at any time in regards to the 'miracle' — which *he also* considers a 'miracle.'

"I sure am depending upon our good Mother Therese of Jesus for the arrival of my new baby."

DOCUMENT OF PHYSICIAN

John S. McIntosh, M.D.
3417 Lake Avenue
Rochester 12, New York

June 16, 1947

To Whom it may concern:

This is to certify that I have attended Mrs. Eldora Scott during three deliveries. With all her babies except the last, she has had long, hard labors. With the last, *Martin Joseph Scott*, the labor only lasted 1 hour and

35 minutes and he was a large baby, weighing 10 lbs. 1 oz.

I consider this case a "miracle" in the sense that it seemed an answer to prayers addressed to God through the intercession of Mother Therese of the Carmel of Allentown, as related by Mrs. Scott. You may use my name at any time to verify this statement.

(Signed) John S. McIntosh, M.D.

From a Sister in New York

On December 26, 1946, Sister M. Dennis, wrote as follows: "Please accept my heartfelt 'God reward you' for your beautiful letter. I was taken back to the hospital again two weeks ago, because pleurisy started to paralyze my lungs. However, through the intercession of Mother Therese, I was home for Christmas.

"So far it is a miracle that I am living. I am grateful for the intercession of our dear Rev. Mother Therese of Jesus."

From Connecticut

Mrs. Alfred B. Wade, of New Canaan, Connecticut, sent the following letter, on April 26, 1947:

"Thank you so very much for your dear letter, and for the little souvenir of dear Mother Therese of Jesus. I am going to send both letter and souvenir to my son so that he and Mme. Belluc and I can start that novena together, beginning on the First Friday of May.

"I hope, God willing, that Mother Therese may give us another miracle!"

FROM A RELIGIOUS IN MASSACHUSETTS

Sister M. Frances, from Massachusetts penned the following letter, on June 20, 1947:

"I made a second Novena through Mother Therese's intercession. It ended on the Feast of the Trinity. I have worn the 'souvenir' right along. However, I look on it in this light: that He might wish Mother Therese's virtue to be made known, and I would be happy to be used as one of the instruments . . .

"On Sunday, I am to enter the hospital for the operations. I still feel that all is to come out all right."

And on July 30, 1947, the same Religious wrote again: "Are you wondering why you have not heard from me? You will surely realize I leaned very hard on the confidence I placed in the care of dear Mother Therese.

"I wore her 'souvenir,' and I asked her to stand at the foot of the bed throughout the siege which, in God's wise plan, was longer than even the Doctor anticipated. Because of Mother Therese, I feel you would wish to know the details. You told me to have no fear, and therefore, I was quietly confident throughout.

"The first operation was performed on the right eye, on Monday, June 23. After a few days, acute conjunctivitis developed. This delayed the second operation until Saturday, July 5th. On that day, I was brought to the operating room, all preparations were made on the left eye which refused to respond as was required for an operation. After an hour I was brought down again.

"On Tuesday, July 8th, the Doctor tried again. Although the eye did not respond, he went through with the type of operation he had planned. When it was completed, he said, 'It is a clear operation, although everything was against us.'"

From Nesquehoning, Pennsylvania

Mrs. John Cerchiaro, of Nesquehoning, Pennsylvania, writing to the Allentown Carmel, on June 11 1947, related the following cure:

"Our daughter Frances was in a terrible accident and received a severe cut on the knee, that continued to bleed, and the Doctors worked on her over an hour. She had to take penicillin every three hours, during the entire week, as well as the sulfa drug. She had a fever for three days.

"When I received your letter, I gave her the 'souvenir' of the Foundress, Mother Therese of Jesus. I blessed her with it, and started a Novena to the Most Holy Trinity, through Mother Therese's intercession.

I prayed in this manner for nine days, and continued my prayers.

"After a week, the stitches were removed, and in the second week, upon removing the bandages, they found *no* infection, nor broken bone, and she was completely discharged.

"We cannot thank Our Lord and Mother Therese enough."

From Catasauqua, Pennsylvania

Miss Kathryn Sharkey, on August 3, 1947, notified the Carmel of the following favors obtained through the intercession of Mother Therese of Jesus:

> "Cure of a severe eye condition,
> Position obtained,
> Special grace received."

From Emmaus, Pennsylvania

On August 11, 1947, Mrs. Felix Pierog, of Emmaus, Pennsylvania, addressed the following letter to Carmel:

"I made a novena, through the intercession of Mother Therese of Jesus, for my son. He had chicken-pox, and infection set in. Unfortunately, too, I opened one of the boils, and the infection spread.

"I am thankful to Our Lord that He answered my prayers, and I thank you very much for the 'souvenir' of Mother Therese. The boy is well."

From a Client in Philadelphia

Writing to the Carmlites, in behalf of his cousin who was critically ill, Mr. Matthew H. McCloskey, Jr., requested prayers for her relief and restoration of health. In turn, Mr. McCloskey's petition was confided to the intercessory prayers of Mother Therese of Jesus. Moreover, a "souvenir" of Mother Therese was gratefully received by the dear patient. Her ensuing letter reveals the fulfillment of her petition.

"Last August, my cousin, Mr. Matthew H. McCloskey, Jr., wrote to your Carmel in my behalf. Now I am happy to tell you that I am almost completely recovered. I cannot tell you how grateful I am to dear Mother Therese of Jesus for this favor."

(Mrs.) Helen McCloskey Tracey.
October 9, 1947.

From a Religious Superior

Sister Mary Paul, of New York, addressed this letter to the Carmelites, at Allentown, on November 6, 1947:

"Perhaps you will recall that I sent the novena prayers, and the 'souvenir' of your Foundress, Mother Therese, to the person in question, who was suffering with an infection in the jaw-bone.

"I am sure your saintly Foundress was responsible for the surcease of pain during these past months.

191

"Perhaps if we leave everything in her hands, and promise publication if this condition is cured, and God sees fit to grant a miracle, she will incline to our petitions."

Carmelites Work Together

On April 21, 1948, Sister Mary Antonia, of Boston, Massachusetts, wrote as follows:

"It seems a long time that I wrote to you. In the meantime I underwent a very delicate operation.

"Our dear friends in Heaven, Little Therese, and Mother Therese, have been so good to me!"

From a Carmelite Superior

The Very Reverend Father Simon Maria Schmitt, O. Carm., has honored these pages, since it was his masterly pen that gave the book its inspired Preface. This outstanding Carmelite's exemplary zeal contributes to his profound knowledge of ascetical and mystical science.

We quote from his Preface, in order to record, at this point, several favors received by him, through the intercession of Mother Therese.

Para. 2.—" . . . At last, however, I could no longer refuse your wish, considering it to be an act of reverence towards our beloved Mother Therese, as well as a token of personal gratitude for favors I believe to have obtained from Divine Goodness, through her intercession."

Para. 3.—"One great favor came to me very soon after my arrival at her Carmel, and I am still enjoying it. The other I received at the time of my grave illness, during the winter of 1947, when a patient in the Sacred Heart Hospital, at Allentown. Day and night I wore about my neck the 'souvenir' of Mother Therese which you so kindly had given to me, some weeks prior to my hospitalization. Needless to say, it is always with me."

SAINT JOSEPH—CARETAKER
By
Rev. Brother Stanislaus, O. Carm.

We have already hinted at Mother Therese's unique and absolute confidence in Saint Joseph's power with the good God.

The following episode in Mother Therese's life, brought to our attention by an eye-witness, Rev. Brother Stanislaus Reybitz, O. Carm., will substantiate our claim.

Brother Stanislaus writes: "Perhaps by this time you have given up all hope of my satisfying your request. Well, I am going to write about one incident that impressed me most — that was the confidence and trust Mother Therese had in Saint Joseph.

"Mr. Ortwein and I were working on the new building one cold—very cold day in February. I told Frank that I couldn't hold the hammer anymore — it was around ten above zero, so we decided to leave. Just as we were making preparations to leave, Mother Therese met us *with her usual smile*. I explained to Mother why we were leaving and asked why there was no heat.

"Mother answered that there wasn't a speck of coal in the bin, but added, with the utmost confidence: 'We will have some coal very soon.' We asked her how she would obtain the coal. Mother smiled and replied: 'From Saint Joseph . . .'

"The good Mother had hardly finished speaking when one of the Sisters came running up the steps, greatly excited, and said that somebody was trying to get in. She begged Mother to send me out to the gate because there seemed to be an unusual noise at that place, and she was afraid. I opened the big gate and beheld a truck, loaded with coal, parked in the driveway.

"The driver asked: 'Is this the Carmelite Monastery?' 'Yes,' I answered, 'what do you want?'

" 'I have a load of coal for the Sisters,' he replied, 'Hurry, tell me where you want me to put it—I am cold.'

"After proper directions, I opened the inner gate, and the cellar window and showed him where to unload the coal. When the truck was empty, he came to Mother for her signature.

"I remarked that it was most unusual for him to bring coal at this particular time.

" 'We were just closing up the shop when a white-haired old man came and gave us the money to have the coal delivered immediately,' explained the driver—'we don't do this for everybody.

" 'Where are you from,' asked Mother Therese.

" 'Shamokin,' came the reply,—'about eighty miles from here—I have a nice trip before me.'

"He drove off—I closed the gates—then Mother Therese turned to her Sister companion and said: ' . . . Saint Joseph . . . !' "

FROM A GRATEFUL CONVERT

On July 5, 1948, Mrs. C. D. Patterson, a benefactress of the Carmel, brought the following message to the Reverend Mother:

"Each and every member of my family is sure that through the intercession of Reverend Mother Therese, many favors have been granted—three very special ones.

"The first—six years ago—so personal and involved, I cannot put it into words except to say that you all, with the help of Reverend Mother Therese, led us from the darkness of despair into the light of hope . . .

195

"The second—my son and every boy whom I enrolled in your Little Flower Auxiliary, among whom were a Jew and many non-Catholics,—each and every one came back safe. One boy, caught in a fox-hole with five other boys, was the only one to survive, and while injured, came home to get well and strong and finished college this year. Another boy, just eighteen years old, was in the Invasion of Normandy; my nephew was on the 'Ticonderoga'—a boy at the next station was killed out-right; several were in the battle of the Bulge—some were fliers. My son's ship was never hit. When I hear how these boys came through while boys touching them were killed, I am awed.

"Thirdly—last summer—July of 1947—my husband had to undergo a serious and dangerous operation. Our doctor told me the operation would last at least three hours and the outcome doubtful . . .

"It lasted less than one hour and a half. Our doctor, a Protestant—told my son and daughter he never saw anything like it—that it went through with miraculous precision. We all *know* it was the intercession of Reverend Mother Therese that did it.

"We feel particularly privileged to have known the saintly Mother Therese in life, while the Monastery was being constructed."

"Christine D. Patterson"

196

Two special favors were recorded in a letter sent to the Carmel, on June 13, 1948, by Mrs. John Tomasovic, of Emmaus, Pennsylvania:

" . . . When I came to you that afternoon, dear Sisters, my little daughter, Leiana, was critically ill with pneumonia. Her fever was over 103. I continued to offer prayers, as you suggested, and pinned to her clothing the 'souvenir' of Mother Therese. That same evening, the fever left her, and she made known to us that she was hungry, and desired to eat. She was so much better. In fact, if this change had not taken place, she would have had to be hospitalized. But thanks to Rev. Mother Therese of Jesus for her prayers!

"Another favor we received from God, through the intercession of Mother Therese, was this:

"My sister's baby was born prematurely. She weighed only five pounds, and continued to lose. At the hospital she was under constant vigilance. I gave my sister the 'souvenir' of Mother Therese of Jesus, and encouraged her to pray. She touched it to the baby.

"Thanks again, through Mother Therese's intercession, the baby recovered. She has been in excellent health ever since."

From Rosemont, Pennsylvania

Mr. Francis I. Downs, of Rosemont, Pennsylvania, on May 19th, 1947, related the following:

"Mrs. Downs was in a very critical condition after giving birth to a little daughter. The baby's life, too, was despaired of.

"I started the Novena in honor of the Most Holy Trinity, through Mother Therese's intercession, and likewise applied her 'souvenir' to my two loved ones. After, this, there was an instantaneous change for the better.

"In gratitude, I will do all in my power to make Mother Therese better known to others."

From Bethlehem, Pennsylvania

On July 15, 1948, Miss Nellie J. Dwyer, of Bethlehem, Pennsylvania, expressed her thanksgiving as follows. We quote from her letter:

"I can thank God I am able to report that Elizabeth is home from the hospital and getting along fine. Her operation was a success and she feels better both in mind and in body. I ask Mother Therese of Jesus to continue to intercede for her with the Most Holy Trinity that she continues to improve."

And on August 22, 1948, Miss Dwyer directed the following message to the Carmel: "My personal intention was likewise answered, the fulfillment of which I attribute to Mother Therese's intercession with the Most Holy Trinity."

Two Favors Reported

Mrs. Pius Topper, of Philadelphia, writing to the Carmel on September 7, 1948, acknowledged the following:

"I am really happy to say I am sure Ann is improving and I earnestly believe it is just since praying to your dear Foundress, Mother Therese of Jesus. You will remember that I explained to you Ann's critical state of health. Well, for some time now, she did not have the doctor. She feels much better.

(Account of the second favor) "I washed today. The skies were threatening, it looked as if it would rain any minute. I petitioned Mother Therese to ask Jesus for sunshine and wind to dry the clothes. They get soiled if they hang in the rain.

"I am thankful I got the sun and the wind."

From Boyertown, Pennsylvania

"Dear Carmelite Nuns:

"It gives me great pleasure to acknowledge publicly the two great favors I have received through the intercession of dear Mother Therese of Jesus.

"After the birth of my little daughter in 1939, my doctor advised that I absolutely could not carry any more children. I had phlebitis, kidney trouble, and other complications. For over four months I was confined to bed, and, in fact, not expected to live.

"When carrying my last child, in 1947, I visited your Carmel. I made many novenas in honor of the Most Blessed Trinity, confiding in the intercession of your Foundress, Rev. Mother Therese of Jesus, and wore her 'souvenir.

"My baby was born normally, in perfect health, and my own health was entirely satisfactory, thanks to the goodness of God, and the prayers of Mother Therese of Carmel. In fact, I enjoyed such excellent health that I was able to look after the children myself, and also attended to my dear Mother who was ill for about three months.

"I wish to add that our 'miracle' child proved to be a son. Previous to his birth, I underwent a serious operation, the success of which I likewise attribute to the Blessed Trinity, and the help of Mother Therese."

(signed) Mrs. Malcolm Koons

REMARKABLE CURE

(The following was recounted by Mrs. Roger Moll, of Bally, Pennsylvania, on her visit to the Carmel of Allentown, on November 28, 1948.)

"It was four years ago, on September 2, 1944, that I was afflicted with infantile paralysis. I was completely helpless, having lost the use of my arms and legs, and was unable to make the slightest movement by myself. My doctor advised hospitalization.

"I remained in the hospital for over five weeks, but medical science was unable to grant me any relief in my great sufferings and state of complete helplessness.

"My doctor informed me that my case was hopeless and that there was nothing more that could be done for me. I was returned to my home where my sister-in-law had the great goodness to take care of me. It was she who informed me about the Carmel of Allentown. Upon visiting the Carmel, and after relating my case to the nuns, she was invited to offer the novena of prayers to the Most Holy Trinity, through the intercession of Mother Therese of Jesus.

"I, too, offered the same prayers to God and wore the little 'souvenir' of Mother Therese sent to me by the nuns. Not long afterwards, I was able to move my arms and legs which, as I have noted, I had not been able to do for several months.

"In the following month of January, I recovered my health to such an extent that I was able to leave my bed and to walk again. From that time on I continued to improve so that I was able to do my own housework and to take care of my family.

"In gratitude to God and to Mother Therese of Jesus,

I feel bound, as it were, to make known this *very remarkable cure*."

From Auburn, New York

Miss M. Gertrude Cora, in her letter of February 27, 1949, reports the following cure:

" . . . I am still making the novena to the Most Holy Trinity, as you suggested, and I am glad to report that my sinus condition has cleared up. I had feared that it would last on 'til the warm weather. I carry the 'souvenir' of your Mother Foundress in my purse daily . . ."

From Reading, Pennsylvania

The following is an excerpt from a letter penned by the Reverend Father William Hammeke:

" . . . Will you do me a favor and pray for me to the Reverend Mother Therese of Jesus, who is buried in your garden? Since two months I have a very sore throat which is painful in speaking and swallowing. The doctors do not know what it is. I have great confidence in the late Mother Therese. I think and hope that she can help me. The doctors and specialists cannot help me . . ."

From Phillipsburg, New Jersey

Miss Sara B. Walker, of Phillipsburg, New Jersey, wrote to the Carmel of Allentown on April 17, 1949, to relate the following:

"Sometime ago you sent me the souvenir of Mother Therese of Jesus. I applied it to my sore arm for nine days and my sister and I have said the prayers aloud together every night since I called. The swelling went down quite a bit although there is still a difference in both arms. However I will continue to pray."

From Bethlehem, Pennsylvania

On May 3, 1949, Mrs. Helen Ference sent a note to the Carmel from St. Luke's Hospital, Bethlehem, Pennsylvania, from which we quote the following: "I am happy to tell you that there is a change for the better in regard to my health. I will continue with my prayers to the Blessed Trinity, through the intercession of Mother Therese of Jesus."

From Rochester, New York

Again we are pleased to insert herein, several letters of Mrs. Thomas Scott, of Rochester, New York, who writes of additional favors obtained from God through the intercession of Mother Therese of Jesus. On February 26, 1949, Mrs. Scott wrote as follows:

"I include the entire community in this letter as the news I am about to relate will interest you all . . . My father (Mr. James Klein) had a check up with Doctor McIntosh and is found 'completely clear' of any sign of sugar, *despite a lack of the strict diabetic diet.* Doctor is quite amazed and is willing to sign a statement of a 'cure' after two more tests—to be certain.

"We would like to arrange for a Mass of thanksgiving in gratitude to Mother Therese for this great favor. Also, could you, perhaps, find a special item that belonged to dear Mother Therese of Jesus that you could spare to send us to cherish? It would be most welcomed and treasured. We certainly feel that we belong to her and that Mother Therese belongs to us, hence the request."

Then on March 7, 1949, Mrs. James Klein, mother of Mrs. Thomas Scott, sent the following message to the Carmel of Allentown:

"Enclosed please find a thanksgiving gift in honor of Saint Joseph and Mother Therese of Jesus. I wish to say my husband's diabetes has almost been cured—*thanks to Mother Therese of Jesus.*

"Mr. Klein will undergo several more examinations in order to make certain of the 'cure.' "

Mrs. Thomas Scott's letter of May 11, 1949, gives further infromation regarding the 'cure' of the diabetic condition of her father, Mr. James Klein, together with an account of another great favor received from God—through the intercession of Mother Therese of Jesus:

"Since my last letter to you, my father has had several sugar tests and he continues to be free of the diabetic diet and *still no sugar*. Our doctor continues to be amazed and desires to make one or two more tests. We *know* he's been cured—thanks to God, and to Mother Therese.

"And now we credit our good friend, Mother Therese, with another big favor. My mother was suffering most acutely from ulcers of the eyes. You have no idea what she suffered on this account. Together we started a novena of prayer in honor of Mother Therese. Thanks to her—I can say that the ulcers have disappeared."

Prayer

My Lord, JESUS CHRIST, deign to make known Thy gentle spouse, Mother Therese of Jesus, to extend the Reign of the Most Holy Trinity in the souls of men, to increase the glory of Your Immaculate Mother Mary; grant to Mother Therese, I beseech Thee, according to Thy holy Will, the honors of Thy Altar. Amen.

(Three times the Our Father, the Hail Mary, and Glory be to the Father, in honor of the Most Holy Trinity.)

✶ ✶ ✶

Most Holy and Adorable Trinity, Father, Son and Holy Ghost, Infinitely loving and merciful, I confidently direct my petition unto Thee. Humbly and reverently, I beseech Thee to glorify Thy gentle spouse, Mother Therese, whose zealous heart was consumed by a great and constant love in Thy holy service.

With my whole heart, I thank Thee, O Triune-God, for all the graces and blessings Thou hast so lavishly bestowed upon Thy humble handmaid, Mother Therese; for the countless crosses, humiliations, and sufferings, of body and soul, wherewith Thou wast pleased to purify her; for the many difficulties, disappointments and hardships by which means Thou didst adorn her soul with special virtues; for Thy tender love and care of her during her entire life; and for the unbounded happiness wherewith Thou didst reward her for all eternity.

O Adorable and Undivided Trinity, Father, Son and Holy Ghost, if it be for Thine own glory, and for the salvation of souls, vouchsafe to Thy faithful servant, the honors of Thy Altar.

I ask this great grace through the Infinite Merits of my Divine Saviour, JESUS CHRIST, through the intercession of His most sweet Mother, through Saint Joseph, Saint Therese, and the whole Heavenly Court. Amen.

May we please earnestly request all who receive favors in answer to prayers, through the intercession of Mother Therese of Jesus, to notify:

> Carmelite Nuns,
> Carmel of the Little Flower,
> "Saint Therese's Valley,"
> Allentown, Pennsylvania

Epilogue

Dear Reader,

It has been a real joy and a rare privilege to be permitted to "ring the bells" of Carmel for you—and especially, to "ring the bells" of the Carmel of Mother
Therese of Jesus, in the valley of Saint Therese! And
you well know the signification of the "ringing of the
bells" of Carmel—it is, and has been, an invitation to
rest and to pray. "Come apart, and rest awhile,"
sweetly invites The Master, when He desires to commune with your soul, and to have you commune with
Him.

And so, my object in writing this humble history, was
to draw you apart for a while, from your busy life, and
to make you hear the voices from the Mountain of Carmel,—the voices that speak of *love*, and of *prayer*, and
particularly, the gracious voice of the Peerless Mother
of Carmel, whose sweet tone finds an echo in the gentle
voice of Mother Therese. You know well, dear Reader,
the Saviour's Great Commandments. And they are two!
Love of God, which finds its plenitude in the prayerful
heart; and love of the neighbor, which is simply "prayer
in action."

Life is as the sea that laves the ancient shores of Mount Carmel—and a tempestuous sea at that! How often we are tossed about on its waves! How we tremble and grow fearful at the roar of its din and turmoil! Pleasure-seeking, we see no dangers; we go where "even angels fear to tread."

Ah, dear Reader, draw nigh to the shore, to the shore that encircles the serene base of MOUNT CARMEL. "Come apart, and rest awhile!" Behold the brilliance of the light emanating from the holy Mountain. It is the Light of the MOTHER of CARMEL, in whose Sacred Arms is enthroned the LIGHT of the world. May its Divine Rays create a new glow of love in your heart—an increase of that burning, active love for Jesus and for Mary, that love which consumed the heart of Mother Therese.

This is the lesson the life of Mother Therese portrays. She dedicated her whole being and her life-long career to the mission of *love* and the apostolate of *prayer*. And as you hearkened to her voice, in the foregoing pages, have you not caught the melody of *peace* that flooded her soul, the sweet fruit of entire conformity to God's Will; the melody of *praise* and *adoration* of the Triune-God, which was the mainspring of her life-work; and the melody of *absolute trust* and *heroic love*, since she offered to Him, at all times, her complete surrender?

Mother Therese, humble and chaste handmaid of the Lord, stayed within the radiance of the Light of Carmel, having for her most tender Mother, Carmel's resplendent Queen, and for her most loving Spouse, the Eternal King of Ages!

Dear Reader, may you be strengthened by the gentle voice, by the living virtues practiced by Mother Therese. Let her beautiful example and the flaming love of God that consumed her, light your way, and draw you to the refreshing peace of Carmel.

Place your hand in the sure Hand of the most sweet Mother of Carmel, and in that of her faithful child, Mother Therese! Permit your Queen to clothe you in Her royal garb—Her *Brown Scapular*—a safeguard on life's sea, a "sign of salvation!" Dear Reader, you know where the conflict lies. It is a challenge between the love of God, and the call of the world. Will you, therefore, heed the voices echoing from Mount Carmel? How will *you* accept the challenge? Listen to their voices:

"To suffer, or to die!" "To suffer, and to be despised for Thy love, O Jesus." "Not to die, but to suffer!" "Never refuse the good God anything." And Mother Therese's maxims in practice: "First and foremost, God's holy Will." "To forget self!"

Dear child of the Saviour, begin now your mission of love, your apostolate of prayer, so that you may help to fill the world with the "sweet odor" of Christ, with the delicate petals of a life lived according to the pattern given you by the heroes of Carmel, and in particular, by another lovely masterpiece of holiness, the saintly Mother Therese of Jesus.

Challenge the world which too often has challenged you by reflecting the radiant beauty of a chaste life, and of a sincere charity. Thus, the Most Holy Trinity will diffuse choicest blessings upon you, upon souls, and upon the entire world.

Ah, let your holy living tell to all the world, as did the loveable, saintly MOTHER THERESE, how sweet it is to love and to serve GOD.

The Author.

5:15 A.M.—The nuns arise. Within twenty minutes, they assemble in the Choir. The Prioress intones the "Veni Sancti Spiritus," after which is read the morning's Meditation. Then the Lay Sisters go to their appointed place to recite the Pater Noster Office; whilst the Choir Sisters recite the Little Hours of the Divine Office. After this, the bell is rung for the continuation of the morning's Meditation.

7:00 A.M.—Conventual Mass, followed by Thanksgiving, until bell is sounded for breakfast. After their breakfast, the nuns go to their respective tasks.

11:45 A.M.—Bell is rung and all the nuns assemble in Choir for their examination of conscience. (Particular Examen.)

12:00 A.M.—Dinner, after which the nuns return to the Choir for their thanksgiving, and their visit to the Blessed Sacrament. There is an hour's recreation period at noon-time.

2:00 P.M.—Vespers is chanted with organ accompaniment. After Vespers there is Spiritual Reading until three o'clock.

3:00 P.M.—The Sisters kneel in adoration, with arms extended, and say the prescribed prayer to Our Lord, in honor of His expiring on the Cross. From three to six o'clock, the nuns apply themselves to their various duties.

6:00 P.M.—Evening Meditation, including the recitation of the Rosary, and daily Novena Prayers. (In common)

7:00 P.M.—Supper, followed by evening recreation.

7:55 P.M.—Compline is chanted, followed by examination of conscience, and night prayer. After Compline, at the sound of the bell, *Grand Silence* begins, lasting until after Prime of the following morning. (On days when Compline follows Vespers, the *Grand Silence* commences likewise at ten minutes before nine o'clock in the evening.)

9:00 P.M.—Lights out.

11:45 P.M.—The Choir Sisters rise for the mid-night Office of Matins and Lauds. After the Office, these Sisters retire again to their cells, until 5:15 A.M.

The cloistered Carmelite Nuns likewise enjoy the privilege of Perpetual Adoration of the Most Blessed

213

Sacrament (without Exposition). Day and night, without ceasing, the cloistered nuns take turns hour by hour, to kneel in prayer and adoration before Our Lord in the Holy Eucharist.

By

Mother Therese of Jesus, O. Carm.

The following verses were composed by Mother Therese, at Christmas 1921.

On the eve of Advent, the Carmelites have the custom of drawing slips, on which is written "how the Little Infant Jesus will come to you, at Christmas-time." Thus, in 1921, Mother Therese's slip read as follows: "Little Jesus comes to you to be your Reward."

"Dear Holy Child, this Blessed Night,
    O'er Bethlehem's humble Hall,
The Angels sing in Jubilee
    That Christ is born for All.
And Peace restored to sinful earth,
    By Thy most humble, lowly birth,
O Holy Babe, my dearest Lord,
    Thou art my sweet and great Reward.

"I come to sing your charms divine,
    Blest Child, in this poor place,
The tear-drops on Thy Face doth shine,
    Amidst Thy smiles of grace,

215

Thy little arms outstretched so sweet,
　　For souls, Thy loving Heart doth seek.
O let me win them for Thee, Lord,
　　Thou art my sweet and great Reward.

"My prayer, O hear, and grant my plea,
　　My poor, sad Fatherland set free,
O change the heartless enmity,
　　Into a loving charity.
Deign, now, to break her chains of woe,
　　From Thy sweet manger-bed, let flow,
Thy saving grace, O mighty Lord,
　　Thou art my sure and great Reward.

"Remember how in days of old,
　　Compassion filled Thy heart,
For suffering and the downcast low,
　　Relief Thou didst impart.
O dry the tears of little ones,
　　Sustain the Priests, Thy faithful sons,
Thy Virgins help, O dearest Lord,
　　Thou art my eternal great Reward.

"To charm Thy lovely tear-dimmed eyes,
　　Of Virgins, form a crown,
To sing Thy praises without prize,
　　In my loved native town,

For souls of men to intercede,
  Beside Thy cradle, watch, they keep,
To love Thee well, my dearest Lord,
  Thou art my endless great Reward.

"When in my agony, I call,
  O Precious Child, my All!
My eyes are dim, and sightless seek,
  And for my sins, I weep . . .
Then open Heaven's Portals wide,
  The souls I saved, let be my guide,
Lead me to Thee, my kindest Lord,
  Thou art forever my Reward.

"Life's exile o'er, gone all its pain,
  The great reward is paid,
That promised Vision, fair to gain,
  Through Heaven's eternal gate.
My tears Thy Hand shall wipe away,
  United to my own again.
Forever more with Thee, dear Lord,
  I come to Thee, my Great Reward!"

✶ ✶ ✶

LAUS DEO ET MARIAE!